Team Building Exercises

Master the Art of Adaptability to Power Your Learning, Growth, and Resilience in High-Performing Group Bonding Activities

Erica May

© **Copyright 2024 - All rights reserved.**

The content of this book may not be reproduced, copied, or transmitted without explicit written permission from the author(s) or publisher. Doing so would constitute a breach of copyright law and could result in serious legal repercussions for any party participating in the illicit reproduction of the material. Furthermore, due to intellectual rights, it is impossible to duplicate or replace the original work produced by the author(s) or publisher; therefore, the only way to legally gain access to this content is through direct authorization from either party.

The publisher and the author(s) of this book shall not be held accountable in any way for any damages, reparations, ill health, or financial losses that may arise because of the information contained herein, either directly or indirectly. This includes any potential harm, monetary loss, or other consequences from individuals' usage of said information. It is also understood that these individuals will not be able to use this clause to evade legal responsibility for their wrongdoings related to the content provided in this book. The publisher and author(s) will thus be free from all liabilities associated with the publication and distribution of this book.

All trademarks, whether registered or pending, are the property of their respective owners.

Legal Notice

This book is subject to copyright protection and should only be used for personal use. Furthermore, it should not be shared with any other individual or persons for any purpose other than that for which it was initially intended. It is strictly prohibited to amend, reproduce, distribute, utilize, quote, or paraphrase any part of the content within this publication without prior authorization from the writer or publisher. Any violation of these regulations may result in legal action against those who have breached them.

Disclaimer Notice

The presented work is strictly informational and should not be interpreted as an offer to buy or sell any form of security, instrument, or investment vehicle. Furthermore, the information contained herein should not be taken as a medical, legal, tax, accounting, or investment recommendation given by the author(s) or any affiliated company, employees, or paid contributors. In other words, the information is presented without considering individual preferences for specific investments regarding risk parameters. General information does not account for a person's lifestyle and financial objectives. It is important to note that no tailored advice will be provided based on the given information.

Table of Contents

PREFACE 16

Enhancing Team Dynamics: A Practical Guide for Modern Corporate Leaders 16

INTRODUCTION 19

CHAPTER 1: HARNESSING TEAM POWER 22

Why Teams Fail or Flourish: The Crucial Role of Building Effective Teams 22
    The Foundation of Organizational Success 23
    Bridging Gaps in Physical and Cultural Distances 23
    Enhancing Team Dynamics 24
    Communication: The Lifeline of Team Operations 24
    Problem-Solving: Enhancing Capability Through Collaboration 24

The Crucial Role of Team Dynamics in Organizational Success 26

CHAPTER 2: BLENDING THE OLD AND THE NEW 33

Harnessing the Power of Hybrid Team Building 33
    Embracing Change in Team Dynamics 35
    Strategizing for Inclusive Collaboration 35

Creating an Adaptive Team Building Strategy for Dynamic Work Environments 37

Blending the Old and the New: A Dynamic Approach to Team Building 41

Step 1: Assess the Team's Needs and Preferences 41
Step 2: Research and Explore Existing Activities 41
Step 3: Customize and Adapt Activities 41
Step 4: Create a Schedule and Plan 42
Step 5: Communicate and Prepare 42
Step 6: Facilitate the Activities 42
Step 7: Reflect and Evaluate 42
Step 8: Adjust and Evolve 42

CHAPTER 3: BEYOND FUN AND GAMES 44

Rethinking Team Building: More Than Just Fun and Games 44

Challenging Misconceptions: Unveiling the Strategic Power of Team Building 47

CHAPTER 4: MEASURING TEAM BUILDING SUCCESS 53

Is Your Team Building Effective? Measure, Evaluate, and Enhance! 53
    Establishing Clear Objectives 54
    Methods of Evaluation 54
    Informing Future Strategies 55
    Practical Insights for Real-world Application 55
    Empowering Teams for Better Performance 55

Measuring the Impact of Team Building: Clear Objectives and Evaluations 57

Virtual Team Connection Model 59
    Technology Utilization 59
    Communication Effectiveness 60
    Relationship Building 60

CHAPTER 5: FLEXIBILITY AT ITS FINEST............64

Harnessing the Power of Adaptability in Team Building................ 64
    The Importance of Customization 65
    Strategies That Meet Specific Needs.. 65
    Learning from Real-world Applications.. 65

Implement Strategies for Customizing Activities According to Specific Team Needs. 68

Flexibility at Its Finest: Crafting Custom Team Building Activities 72
    Step 1: Assess the Team Composition 72
    Step 2: Research and Select Compatible Activities........................... 72
    Step 3: Adjust Activity Instructions and Objectives 73
    Step 4: Provide Clear Communication 73
    Step 5: Adapt Logistics and Materials... 73
    Step 6: Facilitate Sensitivity and Respect 73
    Step 7: Encourage Reflection and Discussion 74
    Step 8: Continuously Learn and Improve... 74

CHAPTER 6: BUILDING BLOCKS OF TRUST..........75

Unlocking the Power of Trust: A Foundation for Peak Team Performance 75
    The Essential Role of Trust in Teams.. 76
    Crafting Exercises to Build Reliance and Cohesion.......................... 76
    Measuring the Impact of Trust-Building Activities.......................... 77

Trust-Building Exercises to Foster Team Cohesion........................ 79

Building Trust: A Step-by-Step Guide 83
    Understand the Importance of Trust 83
    Identify Trust-Building Objectives 83
    Research Trust-Building Activities.. 83
    Customize Activities for Your Team.. 84
    Prepare the Team and Provide Clear Instructions 84

Facilitate the Trust-Building Exercises 84
Assess and Evaluate Trust-Building Progress 84
Maintain and Reinforce Trust 85

CHAPTER 7: REFLECTIONS AND REACTIONS 86

From Activity to Impact: How Effective Debriefing Transforms Team Dynamics 86
Organizing Effective Feedback Sessions 88
Engaging Teams in Reflective Debriefing 88
Cultivating a Continuous Feedback Culture 88

Engage Teams in Reflective Debriefing to Enhance Learning Absorption. 90
Cultivate a Continuous Feedback Culture to Strengthen Team Dynamics 92

CHAPTER 8: CRAFTING CONNECTIONS FROM AFAR 95

Bridging the Digital Divide: Harnessing Virtual Team Dynamics for Peak Performance 95
Recognizing the Unique Challenges of Virtual Teams 96
Integrating Virtual-Specific Strategies 96
Embracing Technology to Simulate Face-to-Face Interaction 97
Empowering Teams Across Distances 97
Fostering Emotional Connectivity 98
Conclusion 98

Integrating Virtual Team Building into Standard Practices for Cohesive Remote Work 100

CHAPTER 9: EMBRACING DIVERSITY IN DYNAMICS 106

Harnessing the Power of Diversity for Enhanced Team Performance 106
    Why Inclusion Matters..............107
    The Role of Culturally Sensitive Exercises..............107
    Fostering Contribution from Every Corner..............108

Fostering an Inclusive Team Environment for Enhanced Collaboration..............110

CHAPTER 10: MASTERMINDS UNITE: STRENGTHENING PROBLEM-SOLVING..............116

Unlocking Team Potential: A Roadmap to Collaborative Excellence 116
    Empowering Through Critical Thinking..............117
    Engaging Exercises in Problem-solving..............117
    Harnessing Diversity for Unified Solutions..............117

Enhancing Team Dynamics with Engaging Problem-Solving Exercises..............120

Collective Problem-Solving Framework..............122
    Problem Identification Phase..............123
    Ideation Phase..............123
    Solution Development Phase..............123
    Implementation Phase..............124

CHAPTER 11: CUSTOM FIT: SCALING TEAM BUILDING..............127

Why Your Team Building Must Evolve with Your Team..............127
    Adapting to Diverse Team Structures..............128
    Meeting Industry-Specific Needs..............128

Adapting Team Building Activities for Different Sectors and Challenges..............131

Scalability and Customization: The Keys to Effective Team Building 134

CHAPTER 12: THE FEEL-GOOD FACTOR............ 136

Unlocking the Hidden Power of Team Building 136
    Understanding Emotional and Psychological Rewards 137
    The Impact on Morale and Stress 137
    Strategies for a Healthier Work Environment 137

The Impact of Team Building Activities on Reducing Stress and Boosting Morale in the Workplace 140
    The Power of Team Synergy 143

CHAPTER 13: EVOLUTION OF TEAM DYNAMICS 145

Is Your Team Building Strategy Evolving as Fast as Your Team? .. 145
    The Imperative of Continuous Improvement 146
    Strategies for Regular Assessment 146
    Cultivating a Culture of Professional Development 147
    Keeping Activities Fresh and Aligned 147
    Responding to Evolving Team Dynamics 147

Continuous Assessment and Refinement of Team Building Activities 150

CHAPTER 14: THE FUTURE OF TEAM SYNERGY 155

Embracing Tomorrow: How New Technologies Are Redefining Team Building 155
    Embracing Innovative Tools for Enhancing Team Engagement and Synergy 159

EPILOGUE 166

Embracing the Future: A Journey Towards Exceptional Team Synergy 166

CONCLUSION 169

BONUS MATERIAL 172

Your Questions, Answered! 172

1. How Can I Effectively Measure the Success of the New Team-Building Strategies Implemented? 172
2. What Are Some Common Obstacles I Might Face When Trying to Foster a Culture of Continuous Improvement, and How Can I Overcome Them? 174
3. How Do I Encourage Team Members to Provide Honest and Constructive Feedback? 176
4. What Specific Digital Tools Can Be Best Integrated With Traditional Team-Building Methods? 178
5. How Can I Adapt Team-Building Strategies to Suit Remote or Hybrid Work Environments? 179
6. How Can I Address Trust and Mutual Respect Issues When Existing Conflicts Are Present Within the Team? 181
7. How Can I Ensure Communication Remains Open and Effective Across Varying Team Dynamics? 183
8. How Do I Balance Team Members' Differing Strengths and Weaknesses to Create a Cohesive Unit? 185
9. What Early Signs Indicate a Need for Reassessment and Refinement of Team-Building Strategies? 187
10. How Can I Maintain Team Morale and Motivation During Significant Change or Uncertainty? 189
11. How Do I Effectively Manage Team Dynamics When Integrating New Members Into an Existing Team? 191
12. What Role Do Emotional Intelligence and Empathy Play in Successful Team-Building, and How Can They Be Developed? 193
13. How Can I Ensure Personal and Professional Growth Opportunities Are Available to All Team Members Equally? 195

14. What Strategies Can Help Deal With Resistance to Change Within the Team? 197
15. How Can I Leverage Emerging Technologies to Stay Ahead of the Curve in Team Development and Performance Enhancement? ... 199

Welcome to the

Ideas Worth Sharing

Series

My name is Nicholas Bright, and I've spent nearly two decades working as a psychologist specializing in Behavioral Neuroscience and Interpersonal Communication in the US, UK, and Australia. Throughout my career, I've encountered countless stories, experiences, and insights that have shaped my understanding of the human mind and interpersonal interactions.

This series is a collaborative effort, bringing together the experience and expertise of myself and my colleagues: Erica May, Jeff Sharpe, Camila Alvarez, and potentially new faces in the future! We've chosen to write under pen names to respect everyone's privacy and keep the spotlight on the valuable content we offer rather than us as individuals. This decision allows us to freely share our knowledge without the distractions that often come with the limelight. We stand by the authenticity and credibility of the content shared here—our professional integrity remains at the forefront of this series.

We are deeply passionate about our field, and our primary goal is to equip you with practical, research-backed insights that you can implement in your everyday life. Each chapter is designed to inspire and help you better understand yourself and those around you.

We invite you to engage actively with the material: take notes, discuss the ideas with friends and family, and, most importantly, apply the lessons in your daily routine.

1. **Read;** understand what can be done to improve
2. **Reflect;** appreciate your feelings and their origins
3. **Remember;** put your learning into action

Thank you for embarking on this journey of knowledge and growth with us,

Nick

Want to Win Free Books?

Join Our Newsletter!

In this series, we appreciate that someone may find many different books helpful. I certainly know that when discussing sensitive topics like, for example, divorce, we can end up working on grief, anxiety, self-confidence, cognitive dissonance, and lots more. When we encounter a major challenge in life, it is rarely due to one small problem but rather a concoction of our experiences, outlooks, and actions; it's often a deep-rooted issue with many different things we need to uncover and support. We are complicated beings, and we must recognize this. As such, I would love to invite you all to join our newsletter.

In this, I aim to write articles of interest, including excerpts from various books in the series, as well as **vouchers**, **discounts**, and **giveaways**—and of course, no gimmicks or catches. I harbor a deep loathing of companies that offer seemingly amazing deals, only to charge you vast amounts in hidden fees! I vowed to never fall into that trap myself, and any offers I make are designed to be of true benefit and help. If you win a book in a giveaway, I want you to read it with a smile.

Join our newsletter and discover the additional value we can add to your life's curriculum!

Join us at: **www.IdeasWorthSharingSeries.com/newsletter**

See you on the inside!

About the Author: Dr. Erica May

Dr Erica May is a dedicated Clinical Psychologist practising in New York City. She graduated from Syracuse University in New York State, earning her degree in Clinical Psychology. Erica specializes in Cognitive Behavioral Therapy (CBT), Dialectical Behavior Therapy (DBT), and trauma-focused treatments. Her work is deeply rooted in helping individuals navigate complex emotional landscapes, enabling them to lead healthier and more fulfilling lives. Her compassionate approach and expertise have garnered her a reputation as a trusted mental health professional in her local community.

Erica has been friends and has worked with Nicholas Bright, the lead author of the Ideas Worth Sharing series, for many years. Together, they aim to help support a wider community by writing a book series on important topics within Psychology and extending their therapeutic insights and techniques beyond the confines of their practice. This book series will cover various topics related to mental health, including detailed guides on implementing CBT and DBT strategies in daily life, as well as comprehensive approaches to prevention, understanding and healing. By presenting practical exercises and learning through her practice, Erica hopes to make evidence-based psychological concepts more accessible to a broader audience. She aims to empower individuals with the knowledge and tools to manage their mental health proactively and independently, fostering greater resilience and well-being.

Preface

"The way to achieve your own success is to be willing

to help somebody else get it first."

Iyanla Vanzant

Enhancing Team Dynamics: A Practical Guide for Modern Corporate Leaders

In the bustling world of modern corporate dynamics, where the digital and physical realms converge, the essence of team synergy often gets overshadowed by the daily grind. This book manifests the realizations and strategies that have emerged from my journey through the corporate world, tailored specifically for you—the team leader, manager, or HR professional striving to sculpt an environment of collaboration and peak performance within your team.

At its core, this guide is crafted to arm you with a robust set of practical exercises to enhance team dynamics. These exercises are designed to be adaptable, whether your team shares a coffee pot or communicates across continents via screens. They foster connection and inspire collective growth and achievement in in-person and virtual settings.

The inspiration to write this book sprang from witnessing numerous leaders grappling with the challenge of nurturing team cohesion in increasingly diverse and dispersed work environments. I recall a particular instance where a seasoned manager expressed frustration over the disconnect within her remote team. Despite her best efforts, the essence of teamwork seemed lost in translation from digital memos and virtual meetings. It was clear that despite having a wealth of resources on leadership and management, there was a dire need for a concise guide on executing team-building exercises that resonated equally well across all platforms.

This guide is also deeply influenced by cutting-edge research in organizational psychology and real-life success stories from thriving companies worldwide. Moreover, invaluable insights were provided by colleagues who have mastered the art of remote team management, which have been integrated into each chapter to ensure you receive the most practical and effective advice.

I am genuinely grateful that you've chosen to engage with this work. Your commitment as a reader honors the efforts poured into these pages and reflects your dedication to enhancing your team's welfare and productivity. By turning these pages, you are taking a pivotal step towards transforming your team's dynamic and unlocking new levels of potential.

This book is intended for proactive leaders like you who are ready to dive deep into team-building mechanics. There are no prerequisites other than a willingness to learn and an open mind toward implementing new strategies.

As you embark on this journey through the book, remember that each exercise and piece of advice is a stepping stone towards creating an environment where every team member can thrive. Thank you for trusting this resource, and I invite you to continue reading, apply these strategies, and witness the transformation within your team unfold.

Introduction

"Change is the end result of all true learning."

Leo Buscaglia

Welcome to a comprehensive guide to elevate your team's synergy and performance. As you embark on this journey, you will find valuable insights and practical tools to transform team dynamics in physical and virtual environments. This guide is crafted to cater to leaders, managers, and team members committed to building a cohesive, high-performing group capable of navigating the complexities of modern workspaces.

In today's fast-paced world, effective teamwork is more critical than ever. With the advent of remote work and global teams, traditional team-building strategies must be adapted and enhanced. This guide delves deep into time-tested methods and innovative techniques leveraging technological advancements. By understanding the intricacies of team dynamics and the importance of trust and communication, you can create a robust framework for team success.

One of the foundational aspects of this guide is the emphasis on trust and mutual respect. These elements are the bedrock of any successful team. Through detailed discussions and case studies, you will learn how to foster an environment where trust flourishes, and every team member feels valued and respected. The strategies outlined here will help you build a culture of openness and reliability that can withstand the challenges of any project or task.

Communication is another cornerstone of effective teamwork. Poor communication can lead to misunderstandings, conflicts, and a lack of cohesion. This guide provides practical exercises and techniques to enhance communication within your team. From improving listening skills to leveraging digital tools for better coordination, you will gain the knowledge to ensure that your team communicates clearly and effectively.

Adaptability is crucial in the ever-evolving landscape of work environments. Whether you are managing a remote team or navigating a hybrid work model, the strategies in this guide will help you remain flexible and innovative. You will explore ways to integrate new technologies seamlessly into your team-building practices and learn how to customize these tools to fit your team's unique needs and dynamics.

Throughout this guide, you will find a mix of traditional team-building activities and cutting-edge virtual solutions. The aim is to provide you with a versatile toolkit that can be adapted to various settings and scenarios. By blending the old with the new, you can create engaging and effective team-building experiences that drive performance and collaboration.

This guide also addresses the importance of continuous learning and development. The journey to achieving peak team performance does not end with implementing new strategies; it requires ongoing effort and adaptation. You will be encouraged to foster a culture of continuous improvement within your team, where feedback is welcomed, and every member is motivated to grow personally and professionally.

To ensure practical implementation, this guide offers step-by-step approaches to assess your team's current dynamics and identify areas for improvement. You will learn how to gather and analyze feedback, make necessary adjustments, and measure the impact of your team-building efforts. By following these steps, you can create a sustainable model for team development that yields long-term benefits.

As you delve into this guide, remember that team dynamics continually evolve. This guide provides a solid foundation and encourages you to stay curious and open to new ideas. Further research and exploration of emerging trends and technologies can offer additional opportunities to enhance your team's cohesion and performance.

Finally, this guide aims to leave you empowered and inspired. Applying the insights and strategies discussed can lead your team to achieve exceptional synergy and success. A team's true strength lies in its ability to grow together, and with the tools provided here, you are well-equipped to navigate this journey.

Chapter 1: Harnessing Team Power

"Progress is impossible without change, and those who cannot change their minds cannot change anything."

George Bernard Shaw

Why Teams Fail or Flourish: The Crucial Role of Building Effective Teams

In today's rapidly evolving workplace, the ability to construct high-functioning teams is more than a beneficial skill—it's an absolute necessity. With the rise of remote work and global collaborations, fostering effective team dynamics has become crucial for any organization aiming for success. This chapter delves into why comprehensive team-building exercises are helpful and essential in modern work environments.

The Foundation of Organizational Success

Organizations thrive on the synergy that well-coordinated teams can achieve. However, creating such teams is not about assembling a group of people and expecting them to work efficiently. It involves intentional and strategic team building to enhance communication, improve problem-solving skills, and foster a collaborative spirit. This chapter explores these elements by providing a roadmap for understanding the underlying principles that make team building indispensable.

Bridging Gaps in Physical and Cultural Distances

One of the paramount challenges today's organizations face is managing teams that are not only geographically dispersed but also culturally diverse. Effective team-building exercises play a pivotal role in bridging these gaps. They help in creating common grounds where mutual respect and understanding flourish. Here, we will preview how such activities are tailored for in-person and virtual settings, ensuring no member feels isolated or misunderstood.

Enhancing Team Dynamics

At the heart of successful teams are robust dynamics that facilitate smooth interactions and an efficient workflow. This section will outline how reinforcing positive team dynamics through targeted exercises can lead to remarkable improvements in how team members relate with one another and work together towards common goals.

Communication: The Lifeline of Team Operations

Clear and effective communication is essential for any team's success. We'll look at how structured team-building activities can significantly enhance this aspect by breaking down barriers to open, honest communication. These exercises are designed to improve how team members talk to each other and how effectively they listen—creating a two-way channel of feedback that is essential for growth.

Problem-Solving: Enhancing Capability Through Collaboration

Every team faces challenges, but the ability to tackle these effectively depends significantly on their collective problem-solving skills. This chapter introduces exercises to boost these skills by encouraging creative thinking and collaborative solutions among team members.

By understanding these foundational aspects, readers will be better equipped to implement practical strategies that enhance teamwork in their organizations. Each exercise and strategy discussed here is backed by real-world applications and research, ensuring you have access to proven methods that can be adapted to your specific organizational needs.

As we progress through this chapter, remember that we aim to understand these concepts theoretically and see their practical implications in everyday scenarios. By fostering an environment where effective teamwork is cultivated, leaders can ensure their organizations are well-prepared to meet the challenges of today's diverse work environment.

Effective team building is a trendy concept and a crucial component of organizational success in today's fast-paced and dynamic work environments. Teams are the backbone of many businesses, and their effectiveness directly impacts productivity, innovation, and employee satisfaction. Understanding why effective team building is essential can pave the way for significant improvements in team performance and overall organizational success.

One of the key reasons why effective team building is essential is its impact on team dynamics. When team members feel connected, understood, and valued, they are more likely to collaborate effectively, communicate openly, and support one another. Strong team dynamics foster a sense of unity and cohesion that can propel a team toward achieving its goals efficiently.

Communication skills are another critical aspect that enhances effective team building. Clear and open communication is vital for resolving conflicts, sharing ideas, and making decisions as a team. Through well-designed team-building exercises, individuals can improve their communication styles, learn to listen actively and express themselves more effectively.

Problem-solving skills are also sharpened through effective team-building activities. Team members develop their critical thinking abilities, creativity, and resilience by working together to overcome challenges and obstacles. These skills are invaluable in navigating complex projects and finding innovative solutions to difficult problems.

Effective team-building exercises are crucial in bridging cultural gaps among dispersed teams in today's diverse workplaces. Whether teams work in the same office or across different time zones, fostering connections and understanding among team members is essential for creating a cohesive and high-performing team.

The Crucial Role of Team Dynamics in Organizational Success

In both in-person and virtual setups, team dynamics play a crucial role in the success of any organization. How team members interact, collaborate, and support each other directly impacts the productivity and morale of the team. Positive team dynamics foster a sense of belonging and create an environment where individuals feel valued and motivated to contribute their best. When team members understand each other's strengths and weaknesses, they can allocate tasks effectively, leading to improved outcomes.

Communication skills are the cornerstone of successful teamwork, whether face-to-face or in virtual environments. Clear and effective communication ensures everyone is on the same page, reducing misunderstandings and conflicts. In-person interactions allow for non-verbal cues like body language and facial expressions to enhance communication. At the same time, virtual setups require more conscious efforts to convey messages clearly through written or spoken words. Developing active listening skills, providing constructive feedback, and encouraging open dialogue are essential components of effective communication within a team.

Problem-solving skills are honed through collaborative efforts within a team. In traditional office settings, team members often gather in meeting rooms to brainstorm solutions, leveraging each other's expertise to tackle complex challenges. In virtual teams, problem-solving may require innovative approaches due to the limitations of physical presence. Encouraging creativity, fostering a culture of experimentation, and promoting a growth mindset are key strategies to enhance problem-solving skills in in-person and virtual teams.

In virtual setups, team dynamics take on a different dimension than face-to-face interactions. Building trust and camaraderie among team members who may never meet in person requires intentional effort. Video calls, instant messaging platforms, and project management tools can help bridge the gap between geographically dispersed team members. Virtual icebreaker activities, regular check-ins, and creating opportunities for informal conversations can strengthen relationships within virtual teams.

Effective communication skills are even more critical in virtual settings with limited non-verbal cues. Clearly articulating ideas, actively engaging in discussions, and practicing empathy in written communication are essential for fostering understanding and collaboration among remote team members. Establishing communication norms such as email response times or video call availability can streamline interactions and prevent misunderstandings.

Problem-solving in virtual teams may require innovative strategies due to the lack of immediate face-to-face collaboration. Leveraging technology for virtual brainstorming sessions, utilizing online whiteboards for idea generation, and encouraging asynchronous collaboration through shared documents can enhance problem-solving capabilities in dispersed teams. Embracing digital tools that facilitate remote teamwork can lead to more efficient solutions and increased productivity.

Organizations can create cohesive teams that excel in achieving their goals by understanding the significance of strong team dynamics, effective communication skills, and proficient problem-solving abilities in traditional and virtual office settings.

Investing time and resources into developing these essential skills will enhance individual performance and elevate the collective success of the team as a whole.

Successful team-building exercises in modern workplaces share key characteristics that make them effective tools for enhancing team dynamics, communication skills, and problem-solving abilities. One crucial aspect is ensuring that the exercises are inclusive and cater to the diverse backgrounds and perspectives within the team. This inclusivity fosters a sense of belonging and encourages all team members to actively participate, regardless of their differences.

Another important characteristic is engagement. The exercises should be interactive, encouraging collaboration and active involvement from all team members. This engagement helps build relationships, trust, and camaraderie among team members, leading to a more cohesive and productive team.

Clear objectives are also essential for successful team-building exercises. Team members should understand the purpose of the activity and how it ties back to the overall goals of the team and organization. Setting clear goals helps in keeping everyone focused and motivated throughout the exercise.

Adaptability is a key characteristic of effective team-building exercises in modern workplaces. Teams today often consist of members from different locations or working remotely, making it crucial for exercises to be adaptable to various settings, including virtual ones. Exercises that can be easily modified to suit different environments ensure that all team members can participate fully.

Feedback mechanisms are vital in successful team-building exercises. Teams need to have opportunities to provide feedback on the exercises, allowing for continuous improvement and refinement. This feedback loop helps tailor future activities to suit the needs and preferences of the team better.

Incorporating elements of fun and creativity into team-building exercises can significantly enhance their effectiveness. Fun activities help break down barriers, reduce stress, and foster a positive atmosphere within the team. Creativity sparks innovation and encourages thinking outside the box, which can lead to new insights and solutions for challenges.

Finally, measuring outcomes is a critical characteristic of successful team-building exercises. Teams should have mechanisms in place to evaluate the impact of the activities on team dynamics, communication skills, problem-solving abilities, and overall productivity. This data-driven approach helps identify areas for improvement and guide future initiatives for continued growth and development within the team.

By incorporating these key characteristics into their team-building exercises, organizations can create impactful experiences that strengthen teams, improve collaboration, and drive success in today's diverse and dynamic workplaces.

As we wrap up this initial chapter, it's clear that effective team building is beneficial and essential for achieving organizational success in today's diverse and often virtual work environments. By understanding the critical role of team dynamics, communication skills, and problem-solving abilities, you can foster a collaborative atmosphere that transcends physical boundaries and cultural differences.

Team building exercises are pivotal in enhancing these skills. They are designed to improve productivity and enrich relationships within a team, making every member feel valued and understood. This foundational step sets the stage for what lies ahead—deeper insights and practical strategies that can be applied directly to your workplace.

The journey through this book promises to arm you with various tools and exercises tailored for both in-person and virtual settings. Each chapter builds on the last, ensuring a comprehensive understanding of how to craft a thriving, dynamic team environment. You will discover innovative ways to engage team members, align their strengths, and propel your organization towards its goals.

Embrace the lessons and strategies discussed here as your first step towards mastering team synergy. With each page, you will gain confidence in your ability to lead and transform your team, ensuring that every group activity contributes positively to overarching business objectives. The potential for growth and improvement is immense, and it starts with the commitment to explore and implement these effective team-building practices.

Remember, the power to mold highly effective teams is in your hands; use it to unlock the full potential of your workforce. As you continue through the book, stay engaged, apply what you learn, and watch your teams transform into powerful engines of innovation and productivity.

Chapter 2: Blending the Old and the New

> "The only way to make sense out of change is to plunge into it, move with it, and join the dance."
>
> **Alan Watts**

Harnessing the Power of Hybrid Team Building

In today's rapidly evolving workplace, integrating traditional and digital team-building exercises has become more than a trend—it's a necessity. As organizations navigate the complexities of a digital work environment, blending old and new methods of team collaboration is essential for fostering effective teamwork and maintaining a competitive edge. This chapter explores how companies can effectively merge these approaches to enhance team dynamics and performance in virtual and in-person settings.

The shift towards a hybrid team-building model acknowledges that while face-to-face interactions are invaluable, the digital components can offer flexibility and inclusivity, bridging geographical distances and schedules. Recognizing this shift is crucial for any organization aiming to cultivate a collaborative culture that leverages the strengths of both traditional and modern practices. By understanding these dynamics, teams can create more engaged, productive, and adaptable work environments.

Creating an adaptive strategy is vital for implementing this hybrid approach. This involves designing innovative team-building activities that include various working situations—whether team members are remote, onsite, or a mix of both. Such strategies ensure that all members feel involved and valued, which is fundamental for nurturing strong relationships and a sense of belonging within the team.

Examples of innovative digital team-building exercises, such as virtual escape rooms, illustrate how technology can engage team members in problem-solving and communication activities. These exercises not only make team building accessible regardless of physical location but also add an element of fun and challenge that can mimic the interactive nature of in-person experiences.

Embracing Change in Team Dynamics

The benefits of integrating these new forms with traditional ones are manifold. They provide teams with varied ways to connect and collaborate, enhancing creativity, better problem-solving, and increasing employee satisfaction. Moreover, by fostering an environment where innovation is encouraged, organizations can stay ahead in adapting to future changes in work patterns.

However, adopting these integrated strategies requires careful planning and openness to experimentation. It involves trial and error, collection of feedback, and continuous improvement to find what best suits a team's needs. It's about creating a balance where technology enhances human interaction instead of replacing it.

Strategizing for Inclusive Collaboration

As we delve deeper into this chapter, we will explore practical ways to implement these hybrid strategies effectively. The goal is not only to adapt but also to thrive in this new era of workplace collaboration. By embracing traditional values and innovative tools, teams can achieve greater synergy and unlock peak performance.

This introduction sets the stage for understanding how blending different methodologies can revolutionize teamwork. The following sections will provide more detailed insights into recognizing shifts in team-building practices, creating adaptive strategies suitable for diverse environments, and analyzing successful examples of digital exercises that have significantly impacted team dynamics.

In today's rapidly evolving work landscape, team-building exercises that cater to in-person settings and the digital realm are necessary. There is a noticeable shift towards integrating both traditional and innovative team-building activities to adapt to the changing dynamics of the workplace. As teams become more geographically dispersed and reliant on digital communication, blending old-school methods with new-age approaches is essential to foster cohesion and collaboration among team members.

Recognizing this shift is the first step toward creating a more cohesive and effective team. By acknowledging the importance of incorporating traditional and digital team-building exercises, leaders can ensure that their teams thrive in diverse work environments. This recognition sets the stage for developing an adaptive strategy that combines the best of both worlds.

By embracing a strategy that includes a mix of in-person and virtual activities, teams can bridge the gap between physical distance and digital connections. This hybrid approach allows team members to engage with one another regardless of location, fostering unity and shared purpose. Incorporating various activities, from classic trust-building exercises to interactive online workshops, can help teams build rapport, enhance communication skills, and strengthen relationships.

The key lies in balancing traditional team-building methods emphasizing face-to-face interactions and innovative digital exercises leveraging technology. This balanced approach ensures that teams can connect personally while also mastering the art of virtual collaboration. By combining the strengths of both types of activities, teams can create a cohesive culture that transcends physical boundaries.

Creating an Adaptive Team Building Strategy for Dynamic Work Environments

Creating a strategy that seamlessly incorporates in-person and virtual team-building activities is crucial in today's dynamic work environment. Balancing traditional face-to-face interactions with digital collaboration is essential for fostering strong team dynamics. By blending the old and the new, teams can adapt to the evolving landscape of remote work while reaping the benefits of traditional team-building exercises.

To create an adaptive strategy, assess your team members' unique needs and preferences. Understand their comfort levels with technology and their preferred modes of communication. This insight will help you tailor activities catering to in-person and virtual settings, ensuring maximum engagement and participation.

Consider implementing in-person and virtual activities to cater to your team's different working styles and preferences. In-person activities such as group outings, team lunches, or workshops can foster personal connections and strengthen relationships. On the other hand, virtual activities like online games, virtual escape rooms, or video conferences can help remote team members feel included and engaged.

Open communication is key to successfully integrating in-person and virtual activities into your team-building strategy. Encourage team members to provide feedback on their experiences with different types of activities and use this information to refine your approach. By actively involving your team in decision-making, you can ensure that the chosen activities resonate with everyone.

Flexibility is essential when creating an adaptive strategy that includes in-person and virtual activities. Be prepared to adjust plans based on feedback, availability, or unforeseen circumstances. Embrace change and be willing to experiment with new ideas to keep your team engaged and motivated.

Set goals for each team-building activity, whether in-person or virtual, to ensure they align with your overall objectives. Define what you hope to achieve through each activity, whether it's improving communication, building trust, or enhancing collaboration. This clarity will guide your choices and help measure the effectiveness of your strategy.

Encourage active participation from all team members in both in-person and virtual activities. Foster a culture where everyone feels valued and heard, regardless of their physical location. By creating opportunities for each team member to contribute their unique skills and perspectives, you can harness the full potential of your diverse team.

An adaptive strategy combining traditional and innovative team-building exercises is essential for successfully navigating today's hybrid work environment. By recognizing the importance of blending the old with the new, you can create a cohesive team culture that thrives both in person and virtually. Embrace flexibility, open communication, clear goals, and active participation to ensure your team-building efforts are effective and impactful across all settings.

In today's digital age, team-building exercises have evolved to accommodate the changing dynamics of the workplace. One innovative example of this evolution is the rise of virtual escape rooms. These virtual challenges allow teams to collaborate, communicate, and problem-solve in a fun and engaging setting. Participating in a virtual escape room allows team members to develop their critical thinking and teamwork skills while having an enjoyable experience.

Virtual escape rooms offer a unique way for teams to bond and work together towards a common goal. The challenges presented in these virtual settings require collaboration, creativity, and quick thinking to successfully solve puzzles and escape within a specified time frame. This activity fosters team cohesion and promotes effective communication and strategic planning among team members.

One key advantage of virtual escape rooms is their adaptability to in-person and virtual settings. In a world where remote work is increasingly common, these digital team-building exercises provide a platform for geographically dispersed teams to come together and engage in a shared experience. This adaptability ensures that all team members, regardless of location, can participate in the activity and contribute to the team's success.

By incorporating virtual escape rooms into your team-building strategy, you can create an environment that encourages collaboration, problem-solving, and innovation. These activities challenge team members to think outside the box, work together towards a common goal, and leverage each other's strengths to overcome obstacles. As a result, teams become more cohesive, communicative, and effective in achieving their objectives.

Virtual escape rooms also offer a break from traditional team-building exercises by providing a dynamic and interactive experience that keeps participants engaged throughout the activity. The element of competition and time pressure adds an exciting dimension to teamwork, motivating team members to perform at their best and showcase their abilities in a challenging yet supportive environment.

In today's rapidly evolving workplace, integrating traditional and digital team-building exercises is beneficial and essential. Embracing in-person and virtual settings allows teams to remain connected and engaged, regardless of location. Virtual escape rooms are not merely trendy but pivotal in fostering a cohesive and adaptable team environment.

Blending the Old and the New: A Dynamic Approach to Team Building

Step 1: Assess the Team's Needs and Preferences

Start by understanding the unique dynamics of your team. Gather insights on preferred activities and any logistical constraints. This foundational step ensures that the selected team-building strategies are relevant and inclusive.

Step 2: Research and Explore Existing Activities

Dive into a mix of traditional and digital team-building exercises. The goal is to create a list that aligns with your team's objectives, ensuring each activity is feasible in your chosen format.

Step 3: Customize and Adapt Activities

Select activities that resonate with your team's preferences. Adapt them for in-person and virtual participation, ensuring everyone can engage meaningfully regardless of location.

Step 4: Create a Schedule and Plan

Establish a balanced schedule that alternates between virtual and in-person activities. Planning ahead with clear timelines and roles will streamline execution and enhance participation.

Step 5: Communicate and Prepare

Keep your team informed about upcoming activities. Clear communication about logistics and expectations will help ensure smooth implementation.

Step 6: Facilitate the Activities

Lead the activities with clear instructions and a focus on engaging every team member. Active facilitation is crucial for maximizing the benefits of each session.

Step 7: Reflect and Evaluate

After each activity, take time to reflect with your team. This step is vital for understanding the impact of the exercises and identifying areas for improvement.

Step 8: Adjust and Evolve

Use feedback to refine future activities. Stay adaptable and open to incorporating new trends that might enhance team dynamics.

This structured approach fosters a unified team environment and enhances the flexibility needed in today's diverse work settings. By blending traditional methods with innovative digital solutions, teams can achieve higher levels of engagement and performance. Implementing this adaptive strategy ensures that every remote or onsite member feels valued and connected, paving the way for sustained organizational success.

Chapter 3: Beyond Fun and Games

"Change your thoughts and you change your world."

Norman Vincent Peale

Rethinking Team Building: More Than Just Fun and Games

When discussing team building, the immediate imagery that comes to mind often involves groups engaged in light-hearted activities, perhaps at a retreat or office game day. While fun is undeniable and essential, there's a profound layer to team building that goes beyond just enjoyment. Team building is a strategic tool to enhance professional efficacy and foster colleague cohesion. This chapter delves into how a deeper understanding of team building can transform it from a mere day of fun into a pivotal growth opportunity for any organization.

The misconception that team building is solely for fun can significantly undermine its value. Leaders and managers might occasionally overlook the strategic potential of these exercises, viewing them as obligations to boost morale rather than opportunities to strengthen the team's core skills and relationships. Organizations can harness the true power of team building by dispelling this common misconception.

Strategic goals are central to effective team building. It's not just about creating leisure moments; it's about crafting experiences that align with the organization's broader objectives. Whether improving communication, enhancing problem-solving abilities, or fostering trust, each activity should be purpose-driven. Recognizing this alignment helps design exercises that are engaging and beneficial in achieving business goals.

Innovative team-building exercises are essential in today's diverse work environment. The shift towards remote and hybrid workplaces has only amplified the need for exercises that can operate effectively across physical and digital realms. Designing activities that cater to these varied environments ensures inclusivity and accessibility, allowing every member to participate actively and feel connected, irrespective of their location.

Furthermore, engaging and purpose-driven exercises are more likely to leave a lasting impact. When team members understand the relevance of their activities within the broader context of their work, participation shifts from being perfunctory to being passionate. This transformation is crucial for the exercises, affecting everyday work interactions and the workplace atmosphere.

As we explore these key themes, we aim to equip leaders with the knowledge to craft more meaningful team-building experiences. The goal is to entertain and create platforms for real professional growth. Through strategic planning and thoughtful execution, team building can become a cornerstone of organizational development.

This chapter sets the stage for rethinking traditional perceptions of team-building exercises. By focusing on their strategic importance and designing them with clear objectives, leaders can unlock their full potential as tools for enhancing team performance and workplace dynamics.

Team building activities are often perceived as light-hearted, fun exercises that aim to break the monotony of the work routine. While enjoyment is a vital component of these activities, there is a prevalent misconception that team building is solely about having a good time and playing games. However, the true essence of team building goes beyond mere entertainment; its primary goal is to enhance professional efficacy and foster stronger cohesion within a team.

Fun vs. Strategic Intent: Many mistakenly believe that team-building exercises are only meant for enjoyment and have no real impact on the team's performance. In reality, these activities are carefully designed to address specific aspects of teamwork, such as communication, collaboration, problem-solving, and trust-building. By engaging in structured team-building exercises, individuals can develop essential skills that directly contribute to improved productivity and efficiency in the workplace.

Building Relationships: Another misconception surrounding team building is that it is solely about creating superficial bonds among team members. While fostering camaraderie is essential, the deeper purpose of these activities is to cultivate genuine relationships built on trust, respect, and understanding. Strong interpersonal connections within a team lead to better communication, increased empathy, and enhanced teamwork.

Professional Development: Team building exercises are not just about having fun together; they serve as valuable opportunities for professional development. Through these activities, individuals can hone their leadership skills, improve their problem-solving abilities, and learn how to work effectively in a group setting. Team building encourages continuous learning and growth, contributing to overall success.

Challenging Misconceptions: Unveiling the Strategic Power of Team Building

By debunking common misconceptions about team building and shedding light on its strategic importance, leaders can unlock the full potential of their teams. Let's delve deeper into the strategic goals of team building in enhancing professional efficacy and cohesion.

Moving beyond the surface level of mere fun and games is crucial in team building. While enjoyable activities can create a positive atmosphere, the true essence of team building lies in its strategic goals. The primary aim of these exercises is to enhance professional efficacy and cohesion within a team. By recognizing this fundamental purpose, leaders can design activities that entertain and contribute meaningfully to their teams' growth and development.

Professional efficacy, or the ability of a team to perform effectively and efficiently, is a cornerstone of successful teamwork. Team building exercises play a vital role in honing this efficacy by providing opportunities for members to collaborate, communicate, and problem-solve together. Through carefully crafted activities, individuals can enhance their skills, learn from each other's strengths, and develop a deeper understanding of how to work cohesively towards common goals.

Cohesion, on the other hand, refers to the bonds that tie team members together. Strong cohesion fosters trust, respect, and mutual support among team members, creating a solid foundation for collaboration. Team building exercises strengthen these bonds by promoting open communication, empathy, and camaraderie. When individuals feel connected and valued within their team, they are more likely to work harmoniously towards shared objectives.

Leaders must design team-building activities with intention and purpose to achieve these strategic goals effectively. Tailoring exercises to focus on specific skills or areas that need improvement can significantly impact the outcomes. Leaders can create targeted activities that address these needs directly by identifying key areas for development within the team, such as communication, problem-solving, or conflict resolution.

Moreover, ensuring that team-building activities align with organizational objectives is essential for maximizing their impact. When exercises are designed to reinforce company values, promote teamwork in line with business goals, and enhance overall performance, they become powerful tools for driving organizational success. Leaders must be intentional in selecting or creating activities that resonate with the vision and mission of the company.

By emphasizing the strategic goals of team building—professional efficacy and cohesion—leaders can guide their teams toward greater success and productivity. Recognizing the importance of these goals allows for more purposeful planning and execution of team-building activities that go beyond mere entertainment. When done thoughtfully and strategically, team building becomes a transformative experience that cultivates strong relationships, fosters growth, and propels teams toward peak performance.

When designing team-building exercises, ensuring they are engaging and purpose-driven is essential. Engagement is crucial to maintain participation and enthusiasm among team members, while purpose-driven activities align with the strategic goals of enhancing professional efficacy and cohesion within the team.

One effective way to design engaging team-building exercises is to tailor activities to the preferences and interests of the team members. Consider their unique personalities, skills, and working styles when selecting or creating exercises. This personalization can make the activities more relatable and enjoyable for everyone involved.

Moreover, incorporating elements of challenge into the exercises can boost engagement levels. Challenges encourage participants to push their boundaries, collaborate with their teammates, and develop problem-solving skills. By including a mix of mental, physical, and creative challenges, you can cater to different preferences and strengths within the team.

To ensure that team-building exercises are purpose-driven, it is crucial to align them with the specific goals and objectives of the team or organization. Clearly define what you aim to achieve through each activity, whether it is improving communication, fostering trust, or enhancing collaboration. This clarity helps participants understand the significance of their involvement and how it contributes to overall team success.

In addition to setting clear goals, consider incorporating elements of reflection into the exercises. After each activity, provide time for team members to share insights, lessons learned, and ways to apply new skills in their work environment. Reflection reinforces the purpose behind the exercises and promotes continuous learning and growth within the team.

Another strategy for designing purpose-driven team-building exercises is to focus on developing specific skills or competencies essential for professional success. For example, you could design activities that enhance problem-solving abilities, decision-making skills, or conflict-resolution techniques. By targeting these key areas, you can ensure that the exercises contribute directly to improving workplace performance.

Furthermore, consider incorporating elements of fun into purpose-driven activities. The fun does not detract from the value of an exercise; instead, it can enhance engagement, motivation, and overall enjoyment. Finding a balance between fun and purpose ensures that team-building exercises are effective but also memorable and enjoyable experiences for all participants.

Team building transcends mere enjoyment; it is a vital strategic tool designed to enhance professional efficacy and cohesion within an organization. By dispelling the myths that team building is only about fun, we uncover its true value as a cornerstone of organizational success. This understanding empowers leaders to craft engaging and purpose-driven exercises, aligning with the broader goals of professional development and team synergy.

Effective team building is rooted in the design of activities that foster real-world skills and promote meaningful interactions. These exercises should be viewed as opportunities to strengthen relationships, improve communication, and boost collaborative skills, essential in today's diverse work environment. The strategic incorporation of these elements ensures that team-building initiatives are more than just entertaining—they become transformative experiences that contribute to an organization's overall health and performance.

Leaders and organizers must approach team building with a dual focus: maintaining engagement and ensuring relevance to professional contexts. By doing so, they harness the power of these activities to address specific organizational needs, such as conflict resolution, leadership development, and adaptability. This tailored approach enhances the immediate team-building experience and solidifies its outcomes, leading to sustained improvements in team dynamics and productivity.

Leaders must recognize their role in guiding their teams through these exercises with empathy and clarity. The success of team building efforts hinges on connecting with team members authentically and motivating them towards common goals. This connection fosters a supportive environment where every participant feels valued and understood, further enhancing the benefits of the activities.

By embracing these principles, organizations can effectively leverage team building to achieve peak performance. The commitment to developing well-thought-out, strategically aligned team-building exercises will pay dividends in enhanced teamwork, smoother communication, and a more cohesive work culture. Therefore, leaders are encouraged to actively engage in this process, continuously seeking innovative ways to integrate meaningful team building into their organizational practices for lasting impact.

Chapter 4: Measuring Team Building Success

"In any given moment, we have two options:

to step forward into growth or

to step back into safety."

Abraham Maslow

Is Your Team Building Effective? Measure, Evaluate, and Enhance!

Regarding team building, the real question isn't whether the activities are fun or engaging but whether they effectively enhance team performance and morale. In today's rapidly evolving work environment, both in-person and virtual, understanding and measuring the impact of these initiatives is more crucial than ever. This chapter delves into practical strategies for setting clear objectives, evaluating outcomes, and using insights gained to refine future team-building efforts.

Establishing Clear Objectives

The foundation of any successful team-building activity lies in its objectives. Measuring success becomes a shot in the dark without a clear understanding of your aim. Setting precise, actionable goals not only directs the course of the activity but also provides a benchmark against which to measure outcomes. We'll explore how to define these objectives to align with your overall business or team goals, ensuring that every activity has a purposeful impact.

Methods of Evaluation

Once objectives are set, the next step is determining how to measure them. This involves both quantitative and qualitative evaluations. Different methods offer varied insights into how well the team-building activities work, from surveys and feedback forms to more nuanced discussions and observations. This section will guide you through choosing the right tools for your specific needs, helping you gather valuable data that reflects the true effect of your initiatives.

Informing Future Strategies

The ultimate goal of measuring team building success is continually improving future efforts. By analyzing the data collected from evaluations, you can identify what works and what doesn't. This continuous loop of feedback and improvement fosters growth and adaptation, essential in today's dynamic work climate. We'll discuss using these insights to craft more effective team-building activities that resonate with and benefit your team.

Practical Insights for Real-world Application

It's important to remember that the effectiveness of team-building activities shouldn't just be guesswork. By establishing clear objectives, employing robust evaluation methods, and adapting based on feedback, you can ensure that these exercises deliver tangible benefits. Whether your teams collaborate in person or connect digitally from afar, these strategies are designed to enhance synergy and promote peak performance.

Empowering Teams for Better Performance

Remember that each team is unique; thus, flexibility in approach and adaptability in execution are key. The insights provided here empower you to take control of your team-building processes and mold them according to your specific group dynamics and organizational culture.

Applying these straightforward yet powerful strategies enhances team cohesion and contributes significantly to achieving broader organizational objectives. Let this be your guide to transforming ordinary team interactions into extraordinary collaborative achievements!

Team building activities are essential to fostering strong relationships, enhancing communication, and improving collaboration within a team. However, to ensure the success of these activities, it is crucial to establish clear objectives from the outset. Setting clear objectives helps define the purpose and desired outcomes of the team-building exercises. Team building activities can become aimless without clearly defined goals and fail to deliver the intended benefits.

When establishing objectives for team building activities, it is important to consider the specific needs and challenges of the team. Tailoring objectives to address the unique dynamics and areas for improvement within the team can lead to more targeted and impactful outcomes. Whether to improve trust among team members, enhance problem-solving skills, or boost morale, having a clear objective in mind provides a roadmap for the following activities.

Moreover, clear objectives create a sense of purpose and direction for participants, helping them understand the significance of their participation in the team-building exercises. When team members know what they are working towards and why it is important, they are more likely to engage wholeheartedly in the activities and contribute actively to achieving the desired outcomes.

In addition to outlining objectives related to specific skills or areas of improvement, it is also beneficial to set overarching goals that align with the overall mission and values of the organization. By connecting team-building objectives to larger organizational goals, participants can see how their efforts contribute to the broader success of the company. This alignment fosters a sense of unity and shared purpose among team members.

Furthermore, establishing clear objectives enables effective evaluation of the success of team-building activities. Clearly defining what success looks like upfront makes it easier to assess whether the desired outcomes have been achieved. This evaluation process provides valuable insights into what worked well and what areas may need further attention or improvement in future team-building initiatives.

Measuring the Impact of Team Building: Clear Objectives and Evaluations

Team building outcomes can be effectively measured with clear objectives and evaluations. Contrary to common misunderstandings, the impact of team building on team performance and morale can be quantitatively and qualitatively assessed. This measurement can guide future activities and highlight areas for improvement, ensuring the exercises deliver their intended benefits.

Establishing clear objectives for team building activities is crucial in evaluating their success. Defining what you aim to achieve before engaging in any team-building exercise is essential. Setting specific goals allows for a more focused evaluation afterward. Objectives could include improving communication, fostering trust, enhancing problem-solving skills, or boosting morale. By clearly outlining these objectives, you create a framework for assessment that aligns with the desired outcomes.

To evaluate team building outcomes quantitatively, consider using surveys or questionnaires that gather numerical data on participants' perceptions before and after the activity. These tools can measure changes in attitudes, satisfaction levels, or perceived effectiveness of teamwork. Quantitative data provides concrete metrics that can indicate the impact of team building on various aspects of team dynamics.

Qualitative evaluation, on the other hand, involves gathering feedback through open-ended questions, interviews, or focus groups. This method delves deeper into participants' experiences, allowing for richer insights into the effects of team-building activities. Qualitative data can reveal nuances that quantitative measures might miss, providing a more holistic understanding of the outcomes.

Combining both quantitative and qualitative approaches enhances the evaluation process, offering a comprehensive view of the impact of team building. By analyzing numerical data alongside detailed participant feedback, you can gain a well-rounded perspective on the activities' effectiveness.

Reviewing the data collected objectively is crucial to use evaluations to inform and improve future strategies. Look for patterns or trends that emerge from the evaluation results. Identify areas of strength and weakness in team dynamics or individual skills. By leveraging this information, you can refine future team-building initiatives to address specific needs and enhance overall performance.

Virtual Team Connection Model

The Virtual Team Connection Model comprises three essential layers that enhance collaboration and unity within virtual teams. Each layer plays a unique role, contributing to the overall effectiveness of the model. By understanding the characteristics and interactions of these layers, teams can create a cohesive virtual environment that fosters communication, relationship-building, and technological efficiency.

Technology Utilization

Technology Utilization is the foundation for seamless virtual collaboration in the Virtual Team Connection Model. This layer focuses on identifying and leveraging digital tools that mimic face-to-face interactions as closely as possible. Key characteristics of this layer include ease of use, accessibility, and the ability to facilitate various forms of communication beyond simple text exchanges. By utilizing video conferencing for real-time communication and collaboration platforms for joint work, teams can bridge the gap between physical distance and create a more connected virtual workspace.

Communication Effectiveness

The Communication Effectiveness layer of the model emphasizes the importance of clear, open, and consistent communication within virtual teams. This layer focuses on developing communication protocols that respect time zones, work-life balance, and cultural differences. Techniques such as regular team meetings, 'virtual coffee breaks,' and structured yet flexible communication channels enhance communication effectiveness. By establishing communication norms that promote transparency and understanding, virtual teams can overcome challenges related to distance and time differences.

Relationship Building

Relationship Building is at the core of the Virtual Team Connection Model and is essential for fostering rapport, trust, and a sense of unity among team members. This layer involves creating initiatives and activities designed to strengthen relationships within the team. Virtual team-building exercises, celebrating achievements, and encouraging informal social interactions all build a cohesive team culture. Virtual teams can create a supportive environment where members feel connected and valued by prioritizing relationship-building activities.

Integrating these three layers—Technology Utilization, Communication Effectiveness, and Relationship Building—the Virtual Team Connection Model provides a comprehensive approach to enhancing collaboration within virtual teams. Each layer supports and enhances the others, creating a synergy that promotes effective communication, trust-building, and overall team cohesion.

The dynamics of this model revolve around the interplay between its components. As technology facilitates communication, effective communication practices enhance relationship-building efforts. In turn, strong relationships foster better utilization of technology by creating a positive collaborative environment. This cyclical relationship ensures that each aspect of the model reinforces the others, leading to sustained connection and productivity within virtual teams.

Practically speaking, the Virtual Team Connection Model offers a roadmap for virtual teams to navigate challenges associated with remote work effectively. By prioritizing technology utilization for seamless communication, establishing clear communication protocols for effective interaction, and investing in relationship-building activities for team unity, virtual teams can overcome barriers to collaboration and achieve their goals efficiently.

In summary, the Virtual Team Connection Model provides a strategic framework for enhancing teamwork within virtual environments by emphasizing technology utilization, communication effectiveness, and relationship building. This model allows virtual teams to cultivate strong connections, foster collaboration across distances, and achieve peak performance in remote work settings.

Measuring the success of team-building activities is not just about ensuring everyone has a good time. It's about achieving specific, beneficial outcomes that align with the team's and organization's broader goals. By setting clear objectives at the outset, we can tailor team-building exercises to address specific needs, improve communication, increase trust, or enhance problem-solving skills.

Establishing clear objectives from the beginning is crucial. This clarity guides the entire process and ensures that every activity is purpose-driven. It's not merely about participating; it's about engaging with a goal in mind. When objectives are well-defined, measuring success becomes straightforward and meaningful.

Evaluating outcomes quantitatively and qualitatively gives us a comprehensive understanding of how effective our team-building efforts have been. Quantitative data might come from performance metrics or completion times during exercises, while qualitative feedback can be gathered through surveys or group discussions. This dual approach allows for a balanced view that respects measurable outputs and team members' nuanced, subjective experiences.

Using these evaluations to inform future strategies is perhaps the most critical step. It's not enough to measure and understand; we must act on this knowledge. The insights gained from each team-building session should be used to refine and improve future exercises. This ensures a cycle of continuous improvement, with each session building upon the lessons of the last.

By integrating these practices, teams see where they are succeeding and where they need to focus their efforts to grow stronger. This ongoing cycle of setting goals, evaluating outcomes, and refining strategies creates a proactive environment of continuous improvement and adaptation.

Embrace these strategies as part of your regular team development initiatives. Start small if necessary, but start—with each step, you'll enhance your team's synergy and performance. Remember, the goal is to foster an environment where all team members feel valued and understood, boosting morale and productivity. Engage actively with these processes; you'll see improved teamwork and a stronger, more cohesive organizational culture emerging.

Chapter 5: Flexibility at Its Finest

> "The measure of intelligence is
>
> the ability to change."
>
> **Albert Einstein**

Harnessing the Power of Adaptability in Team Building

In today's rapidly evolving workplace, the ability to adapt team-building exercises to fit diverse teams is not just beneficial; it's essential. As we delve deeper into the nuances of creating a cohesive and efficient team, it becomes clear that a one-size-fits-all approach to team building is often ineffective. Instead, embracing flexibility allows for the design of activities that resonate more personally with each team member, fostering a stronger connection and enhancing overall performance.

The Importance of Customization

Customizing team-building activities to suit different team sizes and cultural backgrounds is more than a courtesy—it's a strategic necessity. This approach ensures that every team member feels valued and understood, crucial for nurturing an inclusive and productive work environment. By implementing strategies that account for these variances, organizations can avoid the pitfalls of generic exercises that may alienate or fail to engage their staff.

Strategies That Meet Specific Needs

Incorporating strategies for customizing activities according to specific team needs maximizes engagement and boosts the exercise's relevance. When team members acknowledge their unique circumstances and challenges, their investment in the activity and its outcomes increases significantly. This tailored approach helps pinpoint areas where synergy can be enhanced and provides clear pathways.

Learning from Real-world Applications

Exploring real-world examples of adaptable team-building exercises offers invaluable insights into what works and doesn't in various settings. These case studies serve as inspiration and practical guides that can be modified to suit different organizational contexts. Whether it's adjusting the complexity of tasks or incorporating virtual elements to bridge physical distances, these examples provide a blueprint for effective adaptation.

Adaptability in team building activities promotes immediate enjoyment and long-term benefits in communication, understanding, and cooperation across diverse groups. The forthcoming sections will explore practical methods to achieve this flexibility, ensuring every team can benefit from tailored, impactful interactions that lead directly to heightened performance and satisfaction.

Focusing on actionable advice and tangible results, this discussion aims to empower leaders and organizers to take proactive steps toward designing more effective and inclusive team-building initiatives. The goal is straightforward: transform every group activity into a stepping stone towards achieving peak performance through enhanced synergy and mutual respect.

Understanding the dynamics of your specific team and applying these adaptable strategies will improve your efforts' efficacy and contribute to a more harmonious and dynamic work environment. Let's move forward confidently, equipped with the knowledge and tools to craft effective and responsive team-building experiences.

Adapting team-building exercises to diverse team sizes and cultural backgrounds is crucial to fostering effective collaboration within a group. Understanding that teams come in various sizes and consist of individuals from different cultural backgrounds is essential in creating activities that resonate with everyone involved. Flexibility in tailoring exercises to fit these unique characteristics ensures that each team member feels included and valued. Team leaders can create a more cohesive and harmonious work environment by acknowledging and embracing this diversity.

One key strategy for adapting team-building exercises to diverse team sizes is to offer scalable activities. Providing options that can be easily adjusted based on the number of participants allows for seamless integration regardless of the team's size. Additionally, being mindful of cultural differences when designing activities is crucial. Ensuring that exercises are respectful and considerate of various cultural norms and values fosters inclusivity and strengthens relationships among team members.

Incorporating elements that celebrate diversity can also enhance the effectiveness of team-building exercises. By integrating components that highlight the unique strengths and perspectives brought by individuals from different cultural backgrounds, teams can leverage this diversity to their advantage. Encouraging open communication and mutual respect further cultivates a sense of unity within the team, fostering a collaborative spirit that transcends cultural boundaries.

Embracing adaptability in team-building activities promotes inclusivity and enhances overall team dynamics. Flexibility in adjusting exercises to accommodate diverse team sizes and cultural backgrounds demonstrates a commitment to valuing each team member's contributions and experiences. By creating an environment where everyone feels seen, heard, and respected, teams can achieve greater synergy and cohesion, improving performance and job satisfaction.

Implement Strategies for Customizing Activities According to Specific Team Needs.

Understanding their dynamics and challenges is key when tailoring team-building activities to meet your team's unique requirements. Begin by conducting a thorough assessment of your team's current state. Identify areas where they excel and struggle, pinpointing the specific needs that must be addressed through team-building exercises.

Engage with your team members in open discussions to gather insights into what they feel would benefit them most. Listen actively to their feedback and concerns, showing them their input is valued and considered in the planning process. Encourage collaborative brainstorming sessions to generate ideas collectively, fostering a sense of ownership and unity among team members.

Customize activities based on your team's preferences and comfort levels. Some teams may thrive in high-energy, competitive environments, while others prefer more introspective, reflective exercises. Adapt the tone and style of activities to align with your team's overall vibe and communication style, ensuring maximum engagement and participation.

Incorporate elements of fun and creativity into your customized activities. Injecting humor and playfulness can help lighten the mood and foster stronger connections among team members. Encourage creativity by allowing space for innovative solutions to problems within the exercises, promoting a sense of autonomy and empowerment among team members.

Consider the diverse learning styles within your team when customizing activities. Some team members learn best through hands-on experiences, while others prefer visual aids or verbal explanations. Provide multiple avenues for participation, catering to different preferences and ensuring all team members can engage effectively with the exercises.

Follow up on customized activities with reflective discussions. Encourage team members to share their thoughts on the experience, highlighting what worked well and areas for improvement. Use feedback to refine future activities, continuously adapting and customizing based on evolving team needs and dynamics.

By implementing these strategies for customizing activities according to specific team needs, you can create impactful and meaningful team-building experiences that resonate with your team on a deeper level, fostering trust, collaboration, and synergy among members.

In real-world scenarios, adaptability in team-building exercises proves invaluable. Let's explore some practical examples that showcase the effectiveness of flexible approaches in fostering teamwork and collaboration. One such example involves a team with members from diverse cultural backgrounds. The team leader incorporated activities emphasizing active listening and empathy to bridge potential communication gaps or misunderstandings. By customizing the exercises to highlight the importance of understanding different perspectives, the team members could build stronger connections and work more cohesively towards common goals.

Another instance where adaptable team building exercises significantly impacted was when the team size unexpectedly changed due to project requirements. Instead of scrapping the planned activities, the facilitator quickly modified them to accommodate the new team dynamics. By adjusting the tasks to suit smaller and larger groups, the team maintained its momentum and strengthened relationships despite the change in composition.

Flexibility in team-building activities is crucial in a fast-paced work environment where priorities shift frequently. For a team facing tight deadlines and high-pressure situations, engaging in quick energizers or icebreakers helped alleviate stress and fostered a sense of camaraderie. These short yet impactful exercises allowed team members to recharge, refocus, and collaborate more effectively on challenging tasks.

One more example where adaptability shone was when a virtual team needed to build rapport and trust despite not being physically together. By leveraging technology and utilizing virtual collaboration tools, the team engaged in interactive exercises that promoted virtual bonding and communication. The team successfully cultivated a sense of unity and connection through innovative approaches tailored to their remote work setup, leading to improved productivity and engagement.

Real-world examples demonstrate how adaptable team-building exercises can address specific challenges teams face in various contexts. Teams can enhance communication, trust, and collaboration by tailoring activities to suit different circumstances, such as cultural diversity, changing team sizes, or virtual environments. These examples underscore the importance of flexibility in creating meaningful experiences that resonate with team members' immediate needs and contribute to overall synergy within the group.

Adaptability in team building is not just a benefit—it's a necessity. The dynamic nature of today's workforce demands exercises as varied and multifaceted as the teams themselves. We ensure these exercises are relevant and effective by tailoring activities to meet the specific needs of different team sizes, cultural backgrounds, and unique workplace environments. This approach enhances team cohesion and respects and celebrates the rich diversity within teams.

Flexibility at Its Finest: Crafting Custom Team Building Activities

Creating successful team-building experiences involves a structured yet flexible approach, ensuring every team member feels included, valued, and engaged. Here's a step-by-step guide to help you adapt team-building activities effectively:

Step 1: Assess the Team Composition

Start by understanding who is on your team. Evaluate factors like size, cultural background, age, and professional experience. Recognizing these elements helps in planning activities that cater to everyone's needs and preferences.

Step 2: Research and Select Compatible Activities

Choose activities thoughtfully. Ensure they are suitable for your team's demographic and psychographic makeup. The goal is to foster an inclusive environment where every participant feels comfortable and motivated.

Step 3: Adjust Activity Instructions and Objectives

Tailor the rules and objectives to fit your team's specific situation. This customization can involve modifying the activity's complexity, duration, or even the materials used, ensuring accessibility for all members.

Step 4: Provide Clear Communication

Communicate the purpose, rules, and expected outcomes of the activities clearly. Highlight the importance of diversity and inclusion within the team dynamics to enhance mutual understanding.

Step 5: Adapt Logistics and Materials

Ensure that all logistical arrangements and materials reflect the needs of your diverse team. This could mean adjusting the physical setup or providing materials in different languages.

Step 6: Facilitate Sensitivity and Respect

Lead activities with an awareness of cultural nuances. Promote an atmosphere where all voices are heard and respected, enriching the team-building experience.

Step 7: Encourage Reflection and Discussion

After each activity, facilitate discussions that allow team members to reflect on their experiences. This is crucial for reinforcing learning outcomes and deepening team connections.

Step 8: Continuously Learn and Improve

Finally, feedback can be used to refine future team-building sessions. Continuous improvement will help you stay effective and responsive to your team's evolving needs.

By following these steps, you create a robust framework for developing team-building activities that are as dynamic as they are effective. This strategy enhances immediate teamwork and builds a foundation for sustained collective success.

We can create environments that foster genuine connections and collaboration through careful planning, clear communication, and continuous adaptation. Remember, the strength of a team lies in its diversity, and the ability to harness this through well-crafted, adaptable team-building activities is what sets exceptional teams apart. In subsequent chapters, let's carry these insights forward as we explore new dimensions of team synergy.

Chapter 6: Building Blocks of Trust

"To improve is to change; to be perfect is to change often."

Winston Churchill

Unlocking the Power of Trust: A Foundation for Peak Team Performance

Trust is not merely a soft skill—it's the backbone of effective team synergy. Trust becomes even more crucial in today's complex work environments, where teams are often diverse and dispersed across different locations, including virtual spaces. The ability to rely on one another without hesitation allows team members to function efficiently and innovatively. This chapter delves into why trust is essential in team dynamics, showcases how specific exercises can build this trust, and evaluates their impact in real-world settings.

The Essential Role of Trust in Teams

At the core of every high-performing team is a strong foundation of trust. Trust enables teams to communicate openly, share responsibilities effectively, and handle conflicts constructively. It fosters an environment where ideas flow freely, and members feel valued and understood. Without trust, teams may struggle with issues like miscommunication, unnecessary competition, or fear of taking risks—all detrimental to achieving peak performance.

Crafting Exercises to Build Reliance and Cohesion

Developing trust doesn't happen overnight; it requires thoughtful effort and tailored activities that resonate with team members' diverse experiences and backgrounds. This chapter will explore various exercises designed to enhance reliance among teammates. These activities range from simple icebreakers encouraging personal sharing to complex simulations requiring teams to solve problems collectively under pressure. The goal is to create a safe space where trust can grow organically through shared experiences and mutual understanding.

Measuring the Impact of Trust-Building Activities

It's crucial not only to implement trust-building exercises but also to assess their effectiveness. This analysis helps ensure that the activities meet their intended goals and provides insights on how they can be improved for even better results. We will look at different methods to evaluate these exercises, from direct feedback from team members to observing changes in team performance over time.

Practicality is key when applying these concepts in real settings—whether your team operates mainly in-person or virtually. The strategies discussed are adaptable and can be tailored to various team structures and dynamics. By the end of this chapter, you'll clearly understand how implementing focused trust-building exercises can transform your team's interactions and output.

This discussion is theoretical and grounded in real-life applications that show tangible benefits. Teams that excel in building and maintaining trust are more agile, innovative, and better equipped to meet the challenges of today's fast-paced work environments.

This chapter sets the stage for transforming theoretical concepts into practical actions that foster a thriving team culture centered around trust. By building this critical element, teams are better positioned to achieve synergistic success beyond individual capabilities.

Trust is the cornerstone of effective team dynamics. It serves as the glue that holds team members together, fostering collaboration, communication, and cohesion. Teams may struggle to work harmoniously without trust, leading to misunderstandings, conflicts, and reduced productivity. Building trust within a team is essential for creating a positive and supportive work environment where members feel safe to express their ideas, take risks, and support each other's growth.

Trust is not just about reliability; it also encompasses vulnerability and honesty. When team members trust each other, they are more willing to be open and transparent about their thoughts, feelings, and challenges. This vulnerability allows for deeper connections among team members, strengthening relationships and increasing empathy. Trust enables teams to weather storms together, facing challenges head-on with a united front rather than falling apart under pressure.

Trust-building exercises play a crucial role in strengthening bonds among team members. These exercises allow individuals to rely on each other's strengths, communicate effectively, and solve problems collaboratively. By engaging in activities that require trust and cooperation, team members learn to depend on one another and develop a sense of unity.

Effective teams are built on a foundation of trust. When team members trust each other, they are more likely to take risks, share feedback openly, and support one another's growth. Trust fosters a sense of psychological safety within the team, allowing individuals to be themselves without fear of judgment or reprisal. This psychological safety is essential for fostering creativity, innovation, and high performance within a team.

Trust-Building Exercises to Foster Team Cohesion

Specific exercises can play a crucial role in building reliance among team members when it comes to fostering trust and cohesion within a team. These exercises create a more cohesive team environment where individuals can count on each other's strengths. One effective exercise is the "Trust Walk," where team members are paired up, with one person blindfolded and the other guiding them through an obstacle course or around the office. This exercise builds trust and enhances communication and reliance between team members.

Another valuable exercise is the "Two Truths and a Lie" game, where team members share two truths and one lie about themselves, and others have to guess which statement is false. This activity encourages openness, vulnerability, and active listening among team members, ultimately fostering deeper connections and understanding within the group. "Team-building scavenger hunts" can also be a fun way to promote teamwork, problem-solving skills, and collaboration while building trust through shared experiences.

"The Human Knot" is a physical activity that requires team members to stand in a circle, reach out, and grab hands with different people across from them. The challenge is for the group to untangle themselves without letting go of each other's hands. This exercise promotes teamwork, communication, patience, and problem-solving skills. "Group problem-solving challenges" can also be incredibly beneficial in building reliance among team members by encouraging collaboration, creativity, and mutual support to overcome obstacles together.

Role-playing scenarios can be another effective way to build trust within a team. By simulating real-life work situations or conflicts, team members can practice active listening, empathy, understanding different perspectives, and working together towards common goals. "Shared decision-making exercises," where team members collectively make decisions on various topics or projects, can also strengthen trust by involving everyone in the process and valuing each member's input.

Incorporating regular team-building activities, in-person or virtually, into the workflow can significantly enhance trust and reliance among team members. These exercises create opportunities for individuals to connect personally, better understand each other's strengths and weaknesses, and develop a sense of unity toward achieving common objectives. By actively engaging in trust-building exercises, teams can cultivate a culture of support, collaboration, and mutual respect essential for peak performance in today's diverse work environment.

Trust-building exercises are a vital component of fostering effective team dynamics. These exercises cultivate reliance and cohesion among team members, creating a more interconnected and supportive environment. However, the true test lies in evaluating the effectiveness of these trust-building activities in real team settings. It is crucial to assess whether these exercises translate into tangible improvements in team collaboration, communication, and overall performance.

One key aspect of evaluating the effectiveness of trust-building exercises is measuring the impact on team relationships. By observing how team members interact with each other after participating in these activities, leaders can gauge whether trust levels have increased. Improved communication, willingness to collaborate, and mutual support indicate that trust-building exercises have strengthened team bonds.

Another important factor to consider is the impact on productivity. Trust is closely linked to efficiency and productivity within a team. When team members trust each other, they are more likely to work together seamlessly, share ideas openly, and support each other in achieving common goals. By monitoring changes in productivity levels post trust-building exercises, leaders can determine if there has been a positive shift in how the team functions.

Feedback from team members is also invaluable when evaluating the effectiveness of trust-building exercises. Gathering insights from individual team members about their experiences during and after the activities can provide valuable information on how these exercises have influenced their perceptions of trust within the team. Listening to their feedback can help identify improvement areas and refine trust-building strategies.

Observing how conflicts are resolved within the team can also serve as a litmus test for the success of trust-building exercises. Trust is essential for navigating conflicts constructively and reaching resolutions that benefit the entire team. Suppose conflicts are handled more effectively, with respect for differing opinions and focusing on finding solutions rather than assigning blame. In that case, it indicates that trust levels have been positively impacted by these exercises.

Lastly, tracking changes in overall team morale and job satisfaction can offer insights into the lasting effects of trust-building activities. A cohesive and trusting team environment often leads to higher job satisfaction and morale among team members. By assessing whether there has been an uptick in morale or a more positive outlook on work within the team post-trust-building exercises, leaders can gauge the long-term benefits of investing in building trust within their teams.

Trust is the cornerstone of all effective team dynamics, and it's clear that teams struggle to achieve peak performance without it. The exercises and strategies discussed in this chapter are not just activities but essential tools that help build and solidify the bedrock of team success. We can create environments where team members feel valued, understood, and connected through understanding, developing, and evaluating trust-building exercises.

Building Trust: A Step-by-Step Guide

Understand the Importance of Trust

Firstly, educating team members about the crucial role of trust enhances their appreciation and commitment to the team. Trust impacts not only morale but also the efficiency and quality of work. Emphasizing this can motivate the team to engage fully in trust-building activities.

Identify Trust-Building Objectives

Clear objectives set the stage for targeted and meaningful interactions. Whether fostering empathy or enhancing reliance among members, setting these goals helps align the team's efforts with the broader organizational objectives.

Research Trust-Building Activities

Choosing the right activities is pivotal. Activities should be effective and resonate with the team's specific makeup. This involves selecting exercises encourage open communication, vulnerability, and mutual support.

Customize Activities for Your Team

Adaptation is key. Customizing activities to fit your team's unique dynamics and needs can significantly increase their effectiveness. This might mean adjusting scenarios to better reflect real-life challenges the team faces or modifying the difficulty level to suit all members.

Prepare the Team and Provide Clear Instructions

Transparency about what to expect and why certain activities are chosen reassures team members and reduces anxiety or resistance. Clear instructions ensure everyone is on the same page and ready to engage fully.

Facilitate the Trust-Building Exercises

Effective facilitation involves guiding activities with sensitivity and attentiveness to the reactions and interactions of team members. This supportive approach helps foster a safe environment where trust can truly grow.

Assess and Evaluate Trust-Building Progress

Regular evaluation helps understand what works and what doesn't, allowing for timely adjustments. Feedback from team members is invaluable as it provides insight into their personal experiences and the overall impact of the exercises.

Maintain and Reinforce Trust

Finally, trust must be reinforced through continuous efforts and integration into daily interactions. Celebrating successes that highlight effective teamwork and trust reinforces the value of these efforts.

This step-by-step guide not only structures but also simplifies the process of building trust within teams. By following these steps, leaders can foster an atmosphere where trust thrives, enhancing team performance and cohesion. Remember, creating a trustworthy environment is a dynamic and ongoing process that requires commitment, understanding, and adaptability from every team member.

Chapter 7: Reflections and Reactions

"Embrace uncertainty. Some of the most beautiful chapters in our lives won't have a title until much later."

Bob Goff

From Activity to Impact: How Effective Debriefing Transforms Team Dynamics

Understanding the critical role of feedback and reflective sessions in team building is essential for any organization aiming to enhance performance and cohesion. These practices are not merely follow-up activities but foundational to embedding the skills learned and fostering a culture of continuous improvement. This chapter delves into why organizing effective feedback sessions, engaging teams in reflective debriefing, and cultivating a continuous feedback culture are pivotal steps toward achieving peak team performance.

Effective feedback sessions serve as the bridge between theoretical learning and practical application. By systematically reviewing team building activities, organizations can ensure that every member understands their role and sees how their contributions propel the team forward. This clarity is crucial in reinforcing team dynamics and preparing the ground for advanced collaborative tasks.

Reflective debriefing goes beyond standard feedback by encouraging deeper introspection and discussion among team members. This process enhances learning absorption by allowing individuals to express their feelings, challenge their assumptions, and openly discuss what worked or didn't during activities. Such openness not only clarifies misunderstandings but also strengthens interpersonal relationships within the team.

Moreover, establishing a continuous feedback culture marks a strategic shift from episodic improvement efforts to an ongoing commitment to excellence. When teams internalize the habit of giving and receiving constructive feedback regularly, it leads to sustained performance enhancement and adaptability. This cultural shift is vital in today's fast-paced work environments, where teams must rapidly assimilate changes and innovate continuously.

Organizing Effective Feedback Sessions

The importance of structure and clarity in feedback sessions cannot be overstated. These sessions should be designed to pinpoint specific behaviors that promote or hinder team success. Feedback becomes a tool for positive change rather than a source of conflict by focusing on observable actions rather than personal traits.

Engaging Teams in Reflective Debriefing

Facilitating reflective debriefing requires skillful moderation to ensure that every team member's voice is heard. Employing techniques such as open-ended questions helps in uncovering insights that might otherwise remain unspoken. This inclusive approach not only bolsters individual confidence but also enhances collective intelligence.

Cultivating a Continuous Feedback Culture

To truly embed a culture of continuous feedback, leadership must lead by example. Leaders should demonstrate their commitment by actively participating in feedback sessions and showing openness to receiving feedback themselves. Regular training on effective communication and feedback techniques will equip all team members with the tools needed to contribute constructively.

In summary, transforming team-building exercises from isolated events into powerful catalysts for team development requires an intentional focus on post-activity processes. By refining how we organize feedback sessions, engage in reflective debriefing, and foster an environment ripe for ongoing dialogue, we can significantly amplify the impact of our team-building efforts. This chapter will explore practical strategies to implement these elements effectively, ensuring that teams are not just going through the motions but growing through them.

After completing team-building activities, it is essential to organize effective feedback sessions. These sessions reinforce the lessons learned during the activities and allow team members to reflect on their experiences. Feedback sessions serve as a platform for team members to share their thoughts, express their feelings, and discuss what worked well and what could be improved. By providing a structured space for feedback, teams can better understand the impact of the exercises on their dynamics and performance.

Reflective debriefing is integral to the feedback process following team-building activities. Encouraging team members to reflect on their experiences helps solidify the lessons learned and fosters a deeper understanding of the skills acquired during the exercises. Through reflective debriefing, teams can identify patterns of behavior, areas for growth, and opportunities for collaboration. This reflective practice enhances learning absorption and ensures that the benefits of team-building activities are fully integrated into the team's dynamics.

To strengthen team dynamics in the long run, cultivating a

continuous feedback culture is paramount. Regular feedback sessions should not be limited to post-activity debriefs but should become a standard practice within the team. By fostering a culture where feedback is encouraged, teams can address challenges proactively, celebrate successes together, and continuously improve their collaboration and communication skills. This ongoing feedback loop contributes to a positive team environment where members feel supported, valued, and empowered to contribute their best.

Engage Teams in Reflective Debriefing to Enhance Learning Absorption.

Reflection is a powerful tool for learning and growth. After engaging in team-building activities, it is essential to take the time to reflect on the experience. Reflective debriefing sessions allow team members to share their thoughts, feelings, and insights from their activities. By engaging in this process, teams can deepen their understanding of the lessons learned and identify areas for improvement.

During reflective debriefing sessions, encourage team members to share their experiences openly. Create a safe space where individuals feel comfortable expressing their thoughts without judgment. This open dialogue fosters trust and strengthens team cohesion. Active listening is key during these sessions; ensure that all team members have the opportunity to speak and be heard.

Facilitate discussions that prompt team members to consider the following questions: What did we learn from this activity? How can we apply these lessons to our work environment? What challenges did we face, and how did we overcome them as a team? Encouraging self-reflection helps individuals internalize the experience and extract meaningful insights that can be applied in future scenarios.

To enhance learning absorption, encourage peer feedback during reflective debriefing sessions. Team members can provide constructive feedback to one another, highlighting strengths and areas for improvement. This feedback loop promotes continuous growth and development within the team. Encourage accountability by setting actionable goals based on the insights gained during the reflection process.

Incorporate structured reflection activities into your team's regular routine. By making reflection a consistent practice, teams can continuously learn and adapt together. This ongoing process of self-assessment and adjustment strengthens team dynamics and fosters a culture of continuous improvement.

By engaging teams in reflective debriefing, you empower them to extract maximum value from their team-building experiences. Encourage open communication, active listening, self-reflection, peer feedback, and structured reflection activities to enhance learning absorption and promote continuous growth within your team dynamic.

Cultivate a Continuous Feedback Culture to Strengthen Team Dynamics

Encouraging a culture of continuous feedback within your team fosters growth, improves communication, and enhances overall performance. By consistently providing and receiving feedback, team members can address issues promptly, celebrate successes, and work towards common goals more effectively. Creating a safe space where feedback is encouraged and valued is crucial in cultivating a culture of openness and transparency.

Regular feedback sessions can help reinforce positive behaviors, address challenges early on, and keep everyone aligned toward the team's objectives. Incorporating feedback into the team's routine becomes a natural part of the team dynamic rather than an occasional occurrence. Setting clear expectations regarding feedback delivery and reception ensures that everyone understands the importance of this practice.

Feedback should be constructive, specific, and actionable. Instead of vague comments or criticism, focus on providing suggestions for improvement or highlighting areas where individuals have excelled. Encourage team members to share their thoughts openly and listen actively to others' perspectives. By fostering a culture where feedback is seen as a tool for growth rather than criticism, teams can build trust and strengthen their relationships.

Regular check-ins between team members and leaders can provide valuable insights into individual progress, challenges, and development opportunities. These interactions serve as opportunities to offer support, guidance, and encouragement when needed. Recognizing achievements during these feedback sessions can boost morale and motivate team members to strive for excellence.

Embrace a growth mindset within your team by viewing feedback as an opportunity for learning and improvement. Encourage team members to seek feedback proactively and use it as a tool for personal and professional development. By fostering a culture where feedback is integral to success, teams can adapt quickly to changing circumstances, overcome obstacles together, and achieve their goals more efficiently.

Regular feedback and reflective debriefing are pivotal in magnifying the effectiveness of team-building activities. By integrating these practices, teams reinforce their learning and deepen their connections, creating a more cohesive and dynamic group environment. Reflecting on and discussing the outcomes of team exercises ensures that the lessons learned are not fleeting but become ingrained within the team's operational fabric.

Organizing effective feedback sessions after each activity provides a structured approach to commend strengths and identify areas for improvement. This practice fosters an atmosphere of openness and trust where team members feel valued and understood. Leaders must facilitate these sessions in a way that encourages honest and constructive dialogue.

Engaging in reflective debriefing helps team members

internalize their experiences. It transforms simple activities into profound learning opportunities, enhancing the overall absorption of key skills like communication, problem-solving, and leadership. This reflective process clarifies the learning points and empowers teams to apply them in their daily interactions and long-term projects.

Cultivating a continuous feedback culture is essential for ongoing development and adaptation. It turns feedback into a regular part of the team's rhythm rather than a one-time event after specific activities. This continuous feedback loop ensures constant learning and improvement, keeping the team agile and responsive to new challenges.

By implementing these strategies, teams can significantly enhance their performance and synergy. Leaders are encouraged to integrate these insights into their regular operations, ensuring every team member feels supported and motivated to contribute their best. Remember, the goal is to perform tasks together and grow together as a cohesive unit, adapting and thriving in any environment.

Embrace these practices confidently and watch as they transform your team's dynamics, leading to heightened performance and more innovative solutions in your diverse and evolving work environment.

Chapter 8: Crafting Connections from Afar

"It is not the strongest of the species that survive,

nor the most intelligent, but the one

most responsive to change."

Charles Darwin

Bridging the Digital Divide: Harnessing Virtual Team Dynamics for Peak Performance

In today's fast-evolving work environment, the shift towards virtual teams has become more than a trend—it's a staple. However, this transition is not without its unique set of challenges. The essence of teamwork, traditionally reliant on face-to-face interactions, must now be cultivated through screens and digital interfaces. This demands adaptation and a strategic overhaul of team-building methodologies to ensure that the core of collaborative success—connection—is not lost in translation.

Recognizing the Unique Challenges of Virtual Teams

Virtual teams often grapple with issues that rarely affect co-located groups. These range from technical glitches to the profound sense of isolation that can creep in due to the physical separation of team members. Identifying these challenges is the first step toward addressing them effectively. By acknowledging the hurdles specific to remote interactions, leaders can tailor their approach to foster a cohesive and motivated team environment.

Integrating Virtual-Specific Strategies

The integration of dedicated virtual team-building strategies is crucial for maintaining synergy. This involves more than just scheduling regular meetings or check-ins. It requires a thoughtful blend of activities and structured interactions designed specifically for remote participants. These strategies help simulate the incidental conversations and bonding moments naturally occurring in an office setting, nurturing a sense of belonging and teamwork.

Embracing Technology to Simulate Face-to-Face Interaction

Leveraging digital tools is key to bridging the virtual and physical interaction gap. Today's technology offers myriad ways to create an engaging, interactive experience that closely mimics in-person interactions. These tools, from collaboration apps to virtual reality setups, build rapport and ensure effective communication within virtual teams.

In this context, team leaders and members must embrace these technologies not as mere substitutes but as potent enhancers of team dynamics. Through the creative use of digital platforms, teams can achieve remarkable levels of engagement and cooperation.

Empowering Teams Across Distances

Empowering remote teams means equipping them with the right tools and the autonomy to use them effectively. When team members feel trusted and valued, their motivation aligns with the team's goals. This empowerment also involves providing clear guidelines and support systems that enable individuals to navigate their roles confidently within a virtual setting.

Fostering Emotional Connectivity

Through thoughtful communication strategies emphasizing empathy and understanding, emotional connections can thrive despite geographical distances. Regular feedback sessions, open forums for sharing personal and professional updates, and recognition programs tailored for virtual settings can all play significant roles in maintaining high morale.

By focusing on these elements, leaders can cultivate an environment where all team members feel included and valued, regardless of their physical location.

Conclusion

As we delve deeper into this chapter, it becomes evident that crafting connections from afar requires intentional efforts tailored specifically toward overcoming the barriers imposed by distance. The strategies discussed here provide a roadmap for any leader or organization aiming to harness the full potential of their virtual teams. By understanding the unique challenges, integrating effective strategies, and utilizing appropriate digital tools, you can ensure that your remote teams are just as connected if they thrive—and even thrive—in today's digital-first workplace.

Virtual teams face unique challenges that can hinder effective collaboration and teamwork. One of the primary obstacles is the lack of physical interaction, which often leads to feelings of isolation and disconnect among team members. Misunderstandings can easily arise without the ability to engage in face-to-face conversations or observe non-verbal cues, affecting trust and cohesion within the team. Additionally, the reliance on digital communication tools can sometimes lead to misinterpretation of tone or intent, further exacerbating communication barriers.

Building rapport and fostering a sense of belonging within a virtual team can be particularly challenging due to the absence of informal interactions that typically occur in a traditional office setting. Watercooler chats, impromptu meetings, and casual gatherings allow team members to bond and build relationships outside work tasks. In a virtual environment, these organic relationship-building moments are limited, requiring intentional efforts to create similar connections remotely.

Establishing clear communication channels is crucial for virtual teams to overcome challenges related to distance and technology. Miscommunication can easily occur when team members are not on the same page regarding expectations, deadlines, or project updates. By implementing structured communication protocols and utilizing tools such as video conferencing, instant messaging platforms, and project management software, teams can enhance transparency and ensure that information flows effectively across all members.

Managing time zones and scheduling conflicts is another hurdle that virtual teams often face. With team members in different regions or countries, coordinating meetings and collaborative sessions becomes a logistical puzzle. Some team members may need to adjust their working hours to accommodate others, leading to potential disruptions in work-life balance. Addressing these challenges requires flexibility, understanding, and proactive planning to ensure all team members feel included and valued.

Integrating Virtual Team Building into Standard Practices for Cohesive Remote Work

Virtual team-building strategies must seamlessly integrate into standard practices to create a cohesive and connected remote work environment. By incorporating dedicated virtual team-building exercises into regular routines, teams can overcome the challenges of distance and lack of face-to-face interaction. One effective way to do this is by starting each meeting with a brief icebreaker or team-building activity. This simple gesture can help set a positive tone for the meeting, foster camaraderie among team members, and encourage active participation.

Another strategy is establishing clear communication channels and guidelines for remote team members. This includes setting expectations for response times, preferred methods of communication, and protocols for sharing information. By creating a structured communication framework, teams can minimize misunderstandings, enhance collaboration, and build trust among members who may not have the opportunity for casual water cooler chats.

Regular check-ins and progress updates are essential components of successful virtual team building. By scheduling weekly or bi-weekly meetings to discuss progress, challenges, and goals, teams can stay aligned and motivated to achieve their objectives. These check-ins also allow team members to support each other, offer assistance, and celebrate achievements together.

Encouraging social interactions beyond work-related tasks is crucial in fostering a sense of community within virtual teams. Organizing virtual coffee breaks, online happy hours, or even virtual team lunches can recreate the informal bonding moments naturally occurring in traditional office settings. These casual interactions help team members get to know each other personally, strengthening relationships and boosting morale.

Incorporating team-building activities into project milestones can also enhance collaboration and teamwork among remote employees. Whether a virtual scavenger hunt, an online escape room challenge, or a collaborative problem-solving task, these activities can inject fun and excitement into the workday while promoting teamwork and creativity. By infusing playfulness into the work environment, teams can foster a positive atmosphere that encourages innovation and mutual support.

Recognizing and rewarding individual and collective achievements is an important aspect of virtual team building. Acknowledging milestones and accomplishments and publicly exceeding efforts within the team can boost morale and motivation. Small gestures like virtual high-fives, shoutouts during meetings, or sending e-gift cards as tokens of appreciation can go a long way in reinforcing a culture of recognition and support within the team.

Creating opportunities for skill-sharing sessions or knowledge exchanges among team members can strengthen bonds within virtual teams. By showcasing individual expertise or offering mini-training sessions on specific topics relevant to the team's goals, members can learn from each other and build respect for each other's skills. This enhances collaboration and fosters a culture of continuous learning and growth within the team.

Integrating dedicated virtual team-building strategies into standard practices is essential for creating a cohesive and engaged remote work environment. By incorporating icebreakers, establishing clear communication guidelines, scheduling regular check-ins, encouraging social interactions, infusing fun activities into project milestones, recognizing achievements, and promoting skill-sharing sessions, teams can overcome distance challenges and build strong connections that improve collaboration and productivity.

Building rapport and fostering connections in virtual teams can be challenging in the digital age. However, with the right tools and strategies, it is possible to simulate in-person interactions effectively. Utilizing digital tools can bridge the gap between team members scattered across different locations, fostering a sense of unity and camaraderie.

Video conferencing platforms are crucial in virtual team

building, enabling face-to-face interactions despite physical distances. Encouraging team members to switch on their cameras during meetings can create a more personal and engaging environment. Seeing each other's facial expressions and body language can help build trust and strengthen relationships within the team.

Virtual icebreakers are another valuable tool for building rapport in remote teams. These quick activities or games can help break the ice, encourage participation, and create a sense of camaraderie among team members who may not have met in person. Icebreakers can range from simple questions about hobbies to interactive activities like virtual scavenger hunts.

Collaboration tools such as shared online whiteboards, project management software, and messaging platforms are essential for enhancing teamwork in virtual settings. These tools enable real-time collaboration, document sharing, and seamless communication, replicating the experience of working together in a physical office space. Encouraging team members to actively use these tools can streamline workflows and enhance productivity.

Virtual team-building exercises, such as online escape rooms, virtual team lunches, or virtual coffee breaks, can inject fun and creativity into remote work environments. These activities allow team members to bond outside work tasks, fostering a sense of community and shared experiences. Leaders can strengthen relationships and boost morale by incorporating these exercises into regular team routines.

Regular check-ins via video calls or instant messaging help maintain open lines of communication within virtual teams. Setting aside time for one-on-one meetings or team huddles allows team members to address concerns, share updates, and support one another. Consistent communication is key to building trust and ensuring everyone feels connected and valued.

Encouraging informal interactions through virtual water cooler chats or casual messaging channels can create spontaneous conversations and relationship-building opportunities. These informal interactions mimic the impromptu exchanges often occurring in physical office spaces, fostering a sense of belonging and camaraderie among remote team members.

Leaders can create a cohesive and connected remote team by leveraging digital tools effectively and incorporating engaging virtual team-building strategies into everyday practices. Building rapport from afar requires intentionality, creativity, and a commitment to nurturing relationships despite the challenges posed by physical distance. Embracing these strategies can lead to stronger teamwork, improved morale, and enhanced productivity in virtual settings.

Crafting connections within virtual teams is necessary and a pivotal strategy for modern organizations. The shift from traditional in-person setups to digital platforms brings unique challenges that demand innovative solutions. By understanding these intricacies, teams can foster a supportive and collaborative environment, even from afar.

Identifying challenges such as reduced non-verbal communication and potential feelings of isolation is the first step toward overcoming them. Acknowledging these hurdles allows team leaders and members to address issues proactively rather than reactively. It's crucial to remember that while the digital divide can seem vast, it is bridgeable with thoughtful approaches that prioritize connection and understanding.

Integrating virtual team-building strategies into everyday practices ensures that every team member feels valued and engaged. Simple actions like regular check-ins and structured virtual social events can make a significant difference. These efforts boost morale and enhance productivity by building a sense of community and belonging.

Utilizing digital tools effectively can simulate the immediacy and warmth of face-to-face interactions. Tools like video conferencing, real-time collaboration software, and virtual whiteboards can recreate the dynamics of an in-person meeting room. By leveraging technology, teams can maintain continuous communication and collaboration, which is essential for fostering strong interpersonal relationships and a cohesive team culture.

As we move forward, the ability to adapt and innovate in virtual team building will distinguish successful teams from the rest. Embrace these strategies with an open mind and a commitment to continuous improvement. Remember, the power to enhance your team's synergy and performance lies in your hands. By applying these insights, you can transform distance challenges into opportunities for growth and connection.

Chapter 9: Embracing Diversity in Dynamics

"Your life does not get better by chance,

it gets better by change."

Jim Rohn

Harnessing the Power of Diversity for Enhanced Team Performance

In today's interconnected and globalized business environment, the composition of teams is more diverse than ever. This diversity brings a rich tapestry of perspectives, experiences, and skills, which can significantly enhance group creativity and problem-solving. However, effectively managing and integrating these diverse elements poses a unique challenge requiring thoughtful and inclusive team-building approaches.

The essence of innovative team building in this context lies in designing exercises that are not only inclusive but also culturally sensitive. By acknowledging and valuing the cultural differences within a team, leaders can foster an environment where all members feel respected and heard. This approach is crucial in ensuring every team member can contribute their best work, ultimately driving them towards peak performance.

Why Inclusion Matters

Inclusion goes beyond mere representation; it ensures that all team members are actively engaged and valued for their contributions. Inclusive team-building practices help dismantle barriers to full participation, which might exist due to cultural misunderstandings or biases. By focusing on inclusion, teams can harness the full potential of their diverse backgrounds to spur innovation and creativity.

The Role of Culturally Sensitive Exercises

Culturally sensitive exercises are tailored to acknowledge and celebrate the varied cultural backgrounds of team members. These activities are designed to accommodate and actively incorporate different cultural perspectives, enriching the team's collective output. Such exercises educate and build mutual respect among team members, foundational for effective collaboration.

Creating a conducive environment where everyone feels

empowered to share their ideas openly involves understanding and addressing the unique dynamics introduced by cultural diversity. It requires leaders to be perceptive and responsive to the nuances of intercultural communication and interaction within their teams.

Practical strategies for implementing these concepts include structured interactions that encourage equal participation, reflection activities that allow members to express how their backgrounds influence their work, and regular feedback loops to ensure all voices are heard and valued.

Fostering Contribution from Every Corner

To truly embrace diversity within a team, it is imperative to create opportunities that encourage contributions from everyone. This involves recognizing each member's strengths and viewpoints and structuring activities that leverage these assets. By doing so, teams can avoid the pitfalls of conformity and groupthink, often stifling innovation and creativity.

Embracing diversity in dynamics is not just about avoiding conflict or fostering peace among team members; it's about actively pursuing a deeper understanding of each other's worldviews to enhance collaboration and effectiveness. The goal is to create a diverse and united team in its pursuit of common objectives through shared understanding and mutual respect.

In summary, as we delve deeper into this chapter, we will

explore how adopting inclusive practices and celebrating cultural differences through well-crafted exercises can transform diverse groups into high-performing teams. The strategies discussed here will provide practical guidance on creating an environment where every member's voice is heard and instrumental in shaping the team's success.

In today's global work environment, teams are becoming increasingly diverse, bringing together individuals from various cultures, backgrounds, and experiences. As a team leader or member, it is crucial to appreciate the significance of inclusive and culturally sensitive exercises to foster cohesion and productivity within such diverse teams. Inclusive team-building exercises play a vital role in creating a sense of belonging and respect among team members, regardless of their differences.

By recognizing the importance of inclusivity, team leaders can ensure that all members feel valued and heard. Culturally sensitive exercises help acknowledge and celebrate the unique perspectives that each team member brings to the table. These exercises promote understanding and cultivate an environment where diverse viewpoints are welcomed and respected. Embracing diversity through inclusive activities can enhance collaboration, creativity, and team performance.

Understanding the cultural nuances within a team is essential for effective communication and collaboration. By incorporating exercises sensitive to various cultural backgrounds, team leaders can bridge gaps and build stronger relationships among team members. Acknowledging cultural differences in team-building activities demonstrates respect for individual identities and fosters a more inclusive work environment where everyone feels valued.

Inclusivity goes beyond acknowledging differences; it involves actively engaging with diverse perspectives and leveraging them to drive innovation and success. Team building exercises that embrace diversity encourage open dialogue, empathy, and mutual understanding among team members. Creating a culture of inclusivity through tailored exercises can break down barriers, build trust, and promote a sense of unity within the team.

As you navigate the complexities of leading diverse teams, remember that embracing inclusion and cultural sensitivity is not just a box to tick but a fundamental aspect of fostering strong team dynamics. You set the stage for collaboration, creativity, and high performance by prioritizing these values in your team-building efforts. Investing in inclusive exercises is an investment in your team's success and growth in today's multicultural work landscape.

Fostering an Inclusive Team Environment for Enhanced Collaboration

In fostering an environment that encourages contribution from all team members, creating a space where every individual feels valued and respected is essential. Acknowledging the unique strengths and perspectives each team member brings can significantly enhance collaboration and innovation within the group. Encouraging open communication and active listening among team members can help ensure everyone's voice is heard and considered.

Empathy plays a crucial role in fostering an inclusive environment. Understanding and empathizing with the experiences, challenges, and perspectives of team members from diverse backgrounds can build trust and strengthen relationships within the team. Showing genuine interest in learning about different cultures, traditions, and values can create a sense of belonging for all team members.

Promoting psychological safety within the team is paramount for encouraging contributions from all individuals. Team leaders should cultivate an atmosphere where members feel comfortable sharing their thoughts, ideas, and concerns without fear of judgment or reprisal. Creating a supportive environment where mistakes are viewed as opportunities for growth can empower team members to take risks and contribute more actively.

Establishing clear goals and expectations for the team can provide all members a sense of direction and purpose. When everyone understands their roles and responsibilities within the team, they are more likely to engage proactively and offer their insights towards achieving common objectives. Regular feedback sessions can also help recognize individual contributions and address any concerns or issues that may arise.

Inclusivity is not just about inviting diverse perspectives; it also involves involving every team member in decision-making processes and problem-solving activities. Encouraging participation from all individuals, regardless of their background or position within the team, can lead to more comprehensive discussions and innovative solutions. Valuing each person's input fosters a sense of ownership and commitment toward shared goals.

As a leader or facilitator, modeling inclusive behavior by demonstrating respect, fairness, and openness in your interactions with team members is crucial. By setting an example of inclusivity, you encourage others to follow suit and create a culture of acceptance and appreciation within the team. Consistently reinforcing the importance of diversity and inclusion can help build a cohesive and high-performing team where every member feels empowered to contribute their best work.

When creating team-building exercises that respect and celebrate cultural differences, it is essential to embrace diversity wholeheartedly. One way to achieve this is by incorporating cultural elements into the activities. For example, if your team comprises members from different countries, you could organize a potluck where each person brings a dish representing their culture. This fosters appreciation for diversity and allows team members to share personal aspects of their backgrounds.

Encouraging open dialogue is another crucial aspect of creating exercises that respect and celebrate cultural differences. Providing a platform for team members to share their experiences and perspectives can lead to greater understanding and empathy within the team. It is important to ensure everyone feels comfortable expressing themselves without fear of judgment.

Incorporating games and activities that highlight various cultures' beauty can be educational and enjoyable for team members. For instance, organizing a trivia game about different countries or cultures can be fun to learn more about each other. This not only promotes cultural awareness but also fosters a sense of camaraderie among team members.

When designing exercises, it is crucial to be mindful of cultural sensitivities. Avoid activities that may inadvertently offend or exclude certain individuals or groups. Always consider your team members' diverse backgrounds and beliefs to ensure the exercises are inclusive and respectful.

Creating exercises that celebrate cultural differences also involves acknowledging and valuing the unique strengths that each individual brings to the team. By highlighting the contributions of team members from different backgrounds, you reinforce the idea that diversity is an asset that enriches the team as a whole.

In addition to incorporating cultural elements into team-building exercises, seeking feedback from team members on their experiences is important. This feedback can help you understand what aspects of the exercises were particularly meaningful or impactful, allowing you to tailor future activities accordingly.

By creating exercises that respect and celebrate cultural differences, you promote inclusivity and understanding within your team and pave the way for enhanced collaboration and creativity. Embracing diversity in dynamics through thoughtful and culturally sensitive activities can lead to a more cohesive and high-performing team where every member feels valued and appreciated for their unique contributions.

Embracing diversity in team dynamics is about acknowledging differences and actively fostering an inclusive environment where every voice is valued and heard. Integrating culturally sensitive exercises into team building enhances our capacity to appreciate and leverage these differences, leading to richer collaboration and more innovative solutions.

Culturally sensitive exercises are essential; they ensure that all team members feel respected and integral to the team's success. When we design activities that acknowledge and celebrate cultural differences, we send a powerful message of inclusion and respect. This approach strengthens interpersonal bonds, boosts morale, and increases engagement across the board.

Moreover, fostering an environment that encourages contribution from all team members is critical. It empowers individuals, giving them the confidence to share unique perspectives that are invaluable in driving the team forward. This inclusive atmosphere cultivates a sense of belonging and commitment, which is essential for long-term organizational success.

Creating exercises that respect and celebrate cultural differences does more than just build a positive team environment; it sets a standard for interactions. This proactive stance on diversity can significantly impact the group's creativity, problem-solving, and decision-making processes.

By implementing these strategies, teams will see improved collaboration and outcomes and position themselves as leaders in building a truly inclusive workplace. Each step towards this goal enriches your team's dynamics and reflects a broader commitment to global cultural competence—an indispensable asset in today's diverse work environment.

Let us move forward with the confidence that we can create spaces where everyone feels valued and our collective differences propel us toward achieving unprecedented success. Let's harness the power of diversity to unleash the full potential of our teams.

Chapter 10: Masterminds Unite: Strengthening Problem-solving

"Change is the law of life. And those who look only to the past or present are certain to miss the future."

John F. Kennedy

Unlocking Team Potential: A Roadmap to Collaborative Excellence

In today's rapidly evolving work environment, the ability to solve complex problems efficiently and effectively stands as a cornerstone of successful team dynamics. This chapter delves into the essence of problem-solving team initiatives that foster critical thinking and enhance team members' collaborative skills.

By introducing structured exercises and dynamic activities, teams can transcend traditional problem-solving approaches and achieve remarkable outcomes.

Empowering Through Critical Thinking

The first key area we explore is the empowerment of teams through the development of critical-thinking skills. In a landscape where decisions need to be swift and sound, equipping your team with the ability to critically analyze and evaluate information is invaluable. This skill set enables team members to navigate challenges with greater autonomy and confidence, leading to more innovative solutions.

Engaging Exercises in Problem-solving

Secondly, we focus on designing engaging problem-solving exercises that are fun and incredibly effective in stimulating the mind. Games such as strategy simulations and real-world scenario puzzles provide practical frameworks for teams to practice and hone their problem-solving techniques. These activities are designed to be inclusive, catering to diverse teams operating in-person and virtually, ensuring no member feels isolated.

Harnessing Diversity for Unified Solutions

Lastly, we discuss how to facilitate the integration of diverse skills and viewpoints into a cohesive problem-solving strategy. Diversity in thought and expertise is a tremendous asset when addressed correctly. By creating channels for open communication and understanding, teams can leverage their collective strengths to overcome obstacles more efficiently than they could individually.

Throughout this chapter, practical strategies will be outlined to help leaders cultivate these skills within their teams. The goal is straightforward: transform potential energy into kinetic energy — turning capability into action.

By embracing these strategies, leaders can ensure their teams are prepared to face challenges and equipped for future complexities. This proactive approach to building problem-solving prowess within teams is essential for maintaining competitiveness and achieving sustained success in any field.

Whether you're leading a small group or managing large-scale projects, these insights will equip you with the tools necessary to foster an environment where collaborative problem-solving thrives. Remember, the strength of a team lies not just in the sum of its parts but in how effectively those parts work together towards a common goal.

In today's fast-paced work environment, teams face many challenges that require quick thinking and effective collaboration. Developing critical thinking and problem-solving skills is crucial for teams to navigate these challenges successfully. Empowering teams to enhance these skills is essential for boosting productivity and achieving common goals.

Encouraging team members to engage in problem-solving activities sharpens their critical thinking abilities and fosters collaboration and unity within the team. By working together to solve complex problems, team members learn to leverage each other's strengths and expertise, leading to more innovative solutions. Empower your teams by allowing them to tackle challenging tasks requiring them to think outside the box and collaborate effectively.

One effective way to develop critical thinking and collaborative problem-solving skills within teams is through engaging exercises like strategy games. These activities challenge team members to think strategically and promote communication, teamwork, and creative problem-solving. Team members can hone their decision-making abilities by participating in such exercises and learn to work together towards a common objective. Encourage your teams to participate in strategy games or activities requiring them to think critically and collaborate with their peers.

Furthermore, combining diverse skills and viewpoints within the team can significantly enhance problem-solving capabilities. Each team member brings a unique perspective and set of skills, which can be leveraged to tackle complex problems more effectively. Foster an environment where diverse ideas are welcomed and valued, encouraging team members to share their insights and contribute to problem-solving.

As a leader, you must provide your team with the necessary

support and resources to develop their critical thinking and collaborative skills. Investing in training programs, workshops, or team-building activities focused on problem-solving can equip your team with the tools they need to excel in challenging situations. Support your teams in their journey toward becoming more adept problem-solvers by fostering a culture of continuous learning and improvement.

Enhancing Team Dynamics with Engaging Problem-Solving Exercises

Designing engaging problem-solving exercises like strategy games is a powerful way to enhance team dynamics and foster critical thinking skills. By incorporating strategy games into team-building initiatives, you can create an environment where collaboration and problem-solving are at the forefront. These games often require teams to work together, communicate effectively, and think creatively to overcome challenges, mirroring real-world scenarios that teams may face in their professional settings. Through these interactive exercises, team members can hone their decision-making abilities, learn to adapt to changing circumstances, and develop a deeper understanding of each other's strengths and weaknesses.

When designing problem-solving exercises, it is essential to consider the specific objectives you want to achieve with your team. Tailoring the games to address particular areas of improvement can make the experience more impactful and relevant for participants. Additionally, incorporating elements of competition can add an extra layer of excitement and motivation, driving teams to perform at their best. By creating a sense of challenge and urgency, strategy games can simulate high-pressure situations that require quick thinking and effective teamwork.

One effective strategy is introducing various problem-solving exercises that cater to the team's different learning styles and preferences. Mixing up the format of the games, such as incorporating puzzles, role-playing scenarios, or simulation activities, can keep participants engaged and motivated throughout the process. By providing diverse challenges, teams can explore various problem-solving approaches and discover new ways of working together.

Encouraging open communication and collaboration during strategy games is crucial for building trust among team members. Emphasizing the importance of listening to diverse perspectives and valuing each team member's contributions can strengthen teamwork and foster a culture of mutual respect. Creating a safe space for experimentation and innovation within the context of problem-solving exercises allows teams to explore different strategies without fear of judgment, leading to greater creativity and resourcefulness.

Incorporating feedback mechanisms into problem-solving exercises is key to maximizing their impact on team development. Encouraging reflection after each game session enables team members to identify areas for improvement, celebrate successes, and collectively strategize for future challenges. By fostering a continuous learning and growth culture, teams can leverage their experiences from these exercises to enhance their problem-solving skills in real-world scenarios.

Overall, designing engaging problem-solving exercises like strategy games offers a dynamic platform for teams to collaborate, think critically, and develop essential skills for success in today's fast-paced work environments. By embracing these interactive activities, teams can strengthen their problem-solving capabilities, deepen their understanding of each other's strengths, and cultivate a supportive atmosphere where innovation thrives.

Collective Problem-Solving Framework

The Collective Problem-Solving Framework offers a structured approach to maximize the problem-solving capabilities of diverse teams. It consists of four key stages: problem identification, ideation, solution development, and implementation. Each stage is supported by specific team-building exercises to enhance the necessary skills for effective problem-solving.

Problem Identification Phase

In the initial phase of problem identification, the focus is on fostering communication and ensuring that every team member's perspective is heard. This phase aims to enhance the team's ability to recognize and articulate the core problem. By engaging in exercises that encourage active listening and open dialogue, team members can collaborate effectively to pinpoint the root cause of the issue at hand.

Ideation Phase

During the ideation phase, creativity and brainstorming take center stage. Team members are encouraged to think outside the box and share their ideas freely without fear of judgment. The exercises in this phase promote innovative thinking and the open exchange of diverse viewpoints. By embracing a culture of creativity, teams can generate various potential solutions to address the identified problem.

Solution Development Phase

In the solution development phase, exercises focus on honing decision-making and consensus-building skills within the team. By evaluating ideas critically and working towards a consensus on the most viable solutions, team members learn how to navigate differing opinions constructively. This phase emphasizes the importance of collaboration and compromise in reaching effective solutions that benefit from diverse perspectives.

Implementation Phase

The final implementation phase involves developing planning and execution skills essential for putting solutions into action effectively. Through targeted exercises, teams can refine their strategies, allocate resources efficiently, and overcome potential obstacles in the implementation process. By preparing thoroughly for execution, teams can ensure that their solutions are implemented successfully and yield tangible results.

By following this comprehensive framework, teams can approach problem-solving methodically while leveraging diverse viewpoints and skills within the team for optimal outcomes. Each stage guides teams toward effective solutions through collaboration, innovation, critical thinking, and strategic execution.

Empowering teams through targeted problem-solving initiatives is essential for nurturing critical thinking and collaborative skills. By integrating strategy games and complex puzzles into team activities, members enhance their ability to work under pressure and leverage their diverse skills and viewpoints effectively. This approach ensures that all team members feel valued and are motivated to contribute their unique insights to collective challenges.

Problem-solving exercises are more than tasks; they allow teams to grow together. When designed thoughtfully, these exercises mimic real-world challenges that require individual and collective effort to navigate. It's crucial that each member understands the importance of their role and feels confident in their contribution. By fostering an environment where everyone can share ideas freely, teams build a foundation of trust and respect that is vital for successful collaboration.

To make the most of these problem-solving activities, facilitators should focus on creating scenarios requiring various skills and perspectives. This makes the task more engaging and highlights the importance of each team member's input. As teams work through these challenges, they develop a deeper understanding of synthesizing different viewpoints into a coherent strategy that aligns with their goals.

Remember, these exercises aim to prepare teams for the complexities of the workplace, where problems often require quick thinking and collaborative solutions. By practicing these skills in a controlled, supportive environment, team members are better equipped to handle whatever challenges they face professionally.

Encouraging teams to engage actively with problem-solving exercises is a powerful way to enhance workplace dynamics and overall productivity. Each challenge faced and overcome together solves immediate issues and strengthens the team's ability to function efficiently and innovatively in the future.

By integrating these practices into regular team development programs, organizations can ensure that their teams are prepared for today's challenges and forging paths toward future success. Thus, embracing these problem-solving initiatives is beneficial and essential for any team aiming to excel in a competitive, diverse work environment.

Chapter 11: Custom Fit: Scaling Team Building

"If you do not change direction,

you may end up where

you are heading."

Lao Tzu

Why Your Team Building Must Evolve with Your Team

In today's rapidly changing work environment, the effectiveness of team-building exercises hinges significantly on their ability to be both scalable and customizable. As organizations diversify and expand, the one-size-fits-all approach becomes increasingly inadequate. This insight is the foundation for enhancing team synergy through innovative team-building strategies tailored to meet distinct industry needs—in a corporate setting, a non-profit organization, healthcare, or educational institutions.

The core idea here is straightforward: team building activities must evolve to effectively address different sectors' unique challenges and dynamics. This is not merely about having fun or bonding but crafting experiences that foster genuine team growth and improved performance. By ensuring these activities are adaptable, we empower teams to overcome sector-specific challenges more efficiently.

Adapting to Diverse Team Structures

Consider the varied landscapes of today's workplaces: a tech startup operates differently from a large educational institution or a healthcare provider. Each has distinct dynamics, goals, and challenges. Recognizing this diversity is crucial in developing team-building exercises that are not only engaging but also beneficial in fostering a cohesive work culture. The necessity for customization allows for interventions that are directly aligned with the intended outcomes of the team or organization.

Meeting Industry-Specific Needs

Furthermore, scalability ensures that team-building strategies can grow and flex with the organization. Whether expanding from a small to a large team or adapting to virtual environments necessitated by global circumstances, scalability means no team gets left behind due to structural changes or growth. It's about ensuring that every member of an organization, regardless of its size or sector, has access to effective team-building tools.

Practical adaptation techniques will be explored, demonstrating how they can effectively be implemented across various industries. From breaking down complex tasks into manageable components in a corporate setting to fostering empathetic communication in healthcare teams, these strategies highlight the importance of precise adjustments tailored to specific operational contexts.

The ultimate goal is to equip teams with the right tools to successfully navigate their unique professional landscapes. Organizations can enhance productivity and workplace harmony by implementing effective adaptations based on team size, industry-specific challenges, and sector dynamics.

In summary, this exploration into scalable and customizable team-building exercises is not just about improving teamwork; it's about creating a resilient framework that supports continuous improvement and adaptation across all levels of an organization. As we delve deeper into practical solutions and strategies in the following sections, keep in mind that the adaptability of your team-building efforts is crucial in maintaining their relevance and effectiveness in meeting your organizational goals.

Scalability and customization are crucial aspects of effective team-building activities. One size does not fit all when fostering team collaboration, communication, and trust. Each organization, whether in the corporate world, the non-profit sector, the healthcare industry, or educational institutions, has unique challenges and dynamics that require tailored approaches to team building. Customizing team-building exercises to suit the specific needs of different sectors ensures that the activities are relevant, engaging, and impactful.

Scalability is essential for adapting team-building activities to different group sizes and dynamics. What works for a small team may not suit a larger group. By designing activities that can be scaled up or down based on the number of participants, organizations can ensure that everyone is actively involved and benefits from the experience. Flexibility in scalability allows teams of varying sizes to engage fully in team-building, promoting inclusivity and cohesion.

On the other hand, customization involves tailoring team-building exercises to address an organization or industry's specific challenges and goals. For example, a corporate setting may focus on enhancing leadership skills and improving department communication, while a healthcare facility may prioritize teamwork and empathy in patient care. Adapting activities to align with the objectives of each sector ensures that team building is not just a generic exercise but a targeted intervention that addresses specific needs.

Incorporating industry-specific scenarios into team-building activities can make them more relatable and impactful for participants. For instance, a sales team may benefit from role-playing exercises simulating client interactions, while an educational institution could use collaborative projects that mimic real classroom challenges. By mirroring real-world situations in the exercises, teams can practice skills and behaviors directly applicable to their work environment.

Effective customization of team-building activities requires a deep understanding of an organization's culture, values, and objectives. By aligning team-building initiatives with the organization's core principles, leaders can ensure that these activities resonate with participants and drive meaningful change within the team. Tailored exercises that reflect the organization's ethos create a sense of ownership and commitment among team members, fostering unity and purpose.

Adapting Team Building Activities for Different Sectors and Challenges

In the corporate world, team-building activities foster collaboration, communication, and employee trust. Adaptation techniques for this sector involve tailoring exercises to address specific challenges teams face in a fast-paced, competitive environment. Customization ensures that activities resonate with employees and align with organizational goals. For example, incorporating problem-solving scenarios relevant to the industry or simulating real-life work situations can enhance the relevance and effectiveness of team-building exercises in a corporate setting.

In the education sector, adaptation techniques focus on engaging students and promoting teamwork in a learning environment. Team building activities can be tailored to suit different age groups, academic levels, and learning styles. Educators can create an interactive and enriching student experience by incorporating fun, creativity, and collaboration. Furthermore, adapting team-building exercises to align with educational objectives can help reinforce key concepts and encourage active student participation.

Customization is essential when implementing team-building activities in diverse industries such as healthcare. This sector focuses on enhancing communication, empathy, and teamwork among healthcare professionals to improve patient care outcomes. By customizing activities that reflect real-life healthcare scenarios, teams can practice effective communication, decision-making, and problem-solving skills in a safe and supportive environment. Tailoring exercises to address the unique challenges healthcare teams face can lead to improved collaboration and patient satisfaction.

For non-profit organizations, adapting team-building activities involves aligning them with their mission, values, and goals. Customizing exercises to reflect the charitable nature of the organization can help inspire teamwork, motivation, and a sense of purpose among volunteers and staff members. By incorporating social responsibility and community service elements into team-building activities, non-profit organizations can strengthen bonds among team members and increase their impact on their communities.

In implementing effective adaptations for team-building activities, it is crucial to consider the unique aspects of your team, including size, industry, and sector-specific challenges. Tailoring your approach to these specific factors can significantly enhance the impact of team-building exercises. One key strategy is to adjust the activities' scale to suit your team's size. Smaller teams may benefit from more intimate and personalized exercises, fostering deeper connections among team members. On the other hand, larger teams might require activities that promote collaboration on a broader scale.

Industry-specific challenges also play a significant role in customizing team-building activities. For example, in a corporate setting, where competition and high-pressure environments are common, activities focusing on problem-solving under stress can be particularly effective. In contrast, in the education sector, where collaboration and creativity are essential, exercises emphasizing teamwork and innovation may yield better results. Understanding the unique dynamics of your industry is crucial in selecting the most relevant team-building activities.

Moreover, sector-specific challenges can greatly influence the effectiveness of team-building exercises. For instance, healthcare teams face intense pressure and emotional strain in their work, making activities that promote empathy and communication especially valuable. Non-profit organizations may benefit from exercises highlighting shared values and missions to reinforce their collective purpose. Adapting team-building activities to address sector-specific challenges can foster greater cohesion and resilience within the team.

When implementing adaptations based on team size, industry, and sector-specific challenges, it is essential to maintain a balance between structure and flexibility. While having a clear plan for the activities is important, being open to adjustments based on real-time feedback and observations can enhance the overall experience for participants. Encouraging open communication throughout the process can also help uncover any issues or concerns that must be addressed promptly.

Regularly assessing the effectiveness of the adapted team-building activities is crucial. Collecting participant feedback and evaluating outcomes against predefined goals can provide valuable insights into what worked well and what areas need improvement. Iterating on the activities based on this feedback loop can lead to continuous enhancement and refinement.

Scalability and Customization: The Keys to Effective Team Building

Scalability and customization are fundamental for crafting effective team-building activities that resonate deeply with the specific needs of different industries and organizations. Whether it's a corporate setting, an educational institution, or a non-profit organization, the ability to adapt team-building exercises to meet unique challenges and dynamics ensures that every participant finds value and relevance in the activities.

Team building is not a one-size-fits-all solution. By exploring the importance of scalability, we have seen that activities can be adjusted in scope to suit large or small groups, promoting inclusivity and ensuring that no member feels overlooked. Customization allows these activities to address sector-specific challenges, from fostering creativity in a tech startup to enhancing communication in a healthcare setting.

Implementing these adaptations requires clearly understanding the team's objectives, the industry's demands, and the cultural context. This approach boosts the effectiveness of the team-building exercises and enhances their impact, fostering a more connected, motivated, and productive team environment.

Encouraging leaders and organizers to engage with these concepts actively is crucial. You can transform standard team-building exercises into powerful tools for development and change within your organization. Integrating scalability and customization into your team-building strategies ensures that every exercise perfectly aligns with your team's needs and goals.

Remember, the ultimate aim is to create an environment where every team member can thrive. Embracing these adaptable strategies will improve your teams' cohesion and efficiency and contribute significantly to their overall success and satisfaction. This chapter has equipped you with the knowledge and tools to make these necessary adjustments—now it's time to implement them.

Chapter 12: The Feel-Good Factor

"Change before you have to."

Jack Welch

Unlocking the Hidden Power of Team Building

The importance of strong team morale cannot be overstated when we consider modern workplaces' myriad challenges, from high turnover rates to burnout. At its core, the value of team-building exercises extends far beyond simple collaboration enhancement. These activities are pivotal in nurturing a workplace atmosphere and fostering employees' psychological well-being and emotional resilience.

Understanding Emotional and Psychological Rewards

It's well-documented that a positive work environment leads to enhanced productivity and job satisfaction. However, the specific psychological rewards that stem from effective team-building strategies are often less visible yet incredibly significant. By engaging in well-structured team-building activities, employees hone their collaborative skills and experience, which boosts morale and decreases stress levels. This chapter will explore how these emotional and psychological benefits manifest and why they are essential for a thriving workplace.

The Impact on Morale and Stress

A significant aspect of this discussion revolves around the direct correlation between team-building exercises and improved workplace morale. Activities that enhance mutual respect, trust, and understanding contribute heavily to a more cohesive work environment. We will explore case studies and research findings highlighting how regular engagement in these activities reduces workplace stress and builds a more supportive team dynamic.

Strategies for a Healthier Work Environment

Effective team-building strategies require thoughtful planning and a clear understanding of the desired outcomes. This segment will offer practical advice on designing activities that fit your team's unique needs and promote ongoing emotional health benefits. From simple daily interactions to more complex problem-solving exercises, the focus will be on creating sustainable practices that maintain high morale and reduce stress among team members.

The subsequent sections of this chapter will provide you with actionable insights into selecting the right kind of activities tailored to your specific organizational culture and team dynamics. Additionally, we will discuss how these strategies can be adapted for in-person and virtual settings, ensuring inclusivity and effectiveness regardless of your team's location.

By prioritizing emotional well-being through strategic team building, organizations can achieve more than just temporary boosts in morale; they can cultivate an enduring sense of community and satisfaction among employees. This enhances overall productivity and positions companies better regarding retention and employee engagement.

In summary, while the immediate benefits of team building, such as improved collaboration, are widely recognized, the deeper psychological impacts sustain long-term success in any organization. Through careful exploration and application of targeted strategies, it's possible to transform everyday teamwork into a powerful catalyst for workplace wellness.

Team building activities offer more than just practical skills; they provide many psychological and emotional benefits that can significantly enhance workplace morale. Beyond the surface level of teamwork and collaboration, these activities can foster a sense of camaraderie, trust, and mutual respect among team members. When individuals feel connected to their colleagues personally, job satisfaction and a more positive work environment can increase.

One of the key psychological benefits of team building is the boost in morale that it can bring. Engaging in activities that are fun, challenging, and require cooperation can uplift spirits and create a sense of accomplishment within the team. This boost in morale can have a ripple effect on overall productivity and motivation, as team members are more likely to approach tasks enthusiastically and positively.

Another significant advantage of team-building activities is their ability to reduce workplace stress. In today's fast-paced and high-pressure work environments, stress levels can run high, leading to burnout and decreased job satisfaction. By providing an opportunity for team members to relax, have fun, and engage in non-work-related activities, team building can help alleviate stress and promote mental well-being.

Moreover, team building fosters better communication and collaboration among team members. When individuals participate in activities that require them to work together towards a common goal, they learn to communicate effectively, listen actively, and leverage each other's strengths. This improved communication can translate into more efficient teamwork in the workplace, leading to better problem-solving, decision-making, and overall performance.

The Impact of Team Building Activities on Reducing Stress and Boosting Morale in the Workplace

In the fast-paced world of modern workplaces, stress can often run high, impacting team morale and productivity. Team building activities can serve as a powerful antidote to this common issue, offering a range of benefits beyond improving teamwork skills. By engaging in these activities, teams can experience a boost in morale and significantly reduce workplace stress, leading to a more positive and cohesive work environment.

Morale is a crucial factor in determining the overall well-being of a team. When team members feel connected, supported, and appreciated, they are more likely to be motivated and engaged. Team building activities provide opportunities for colleagues to bond outside of their usual work tasks, fostering relationships that can translate into improved morale back in the office. Through shared experiences and challenges, team members develop a sense of camaraderie and mutual support that can impact how they interact and collaborate daily.

Reducing workplace stress is another key benefit of engaging in team-building activities. Stress can harm individuals and teams, decreasing productivity, low morale, and even burnout. By participating in activities that encourage communication, problem-solving, and creativity, teams can learn to manage stress more effectively. These activities provide a safe space for team members to relax, have fun, and build trust with one another, creating a positive outlet for releasing tension and promoting mental well-being.

Team building activities also allow teams to leave their daily tasks and focus on building relationships. Amid deadlines and deliverables, it's easy for team members to become siloed in their work. Teams can break down barriers and foster a sense of unity by coming together for structured activities to promote collaboration and communication. This sense of unity strengthens the team and helps individual team members feel supported and valued.

Ultimately, by investing time and effort into team-building activities, organizations can reap the benefits of improved morale and reduced workplace stress. These activities create a positive feedback loop, where happier employees are more engaged, increasing productivity and job satisfaction. By prioritizing the emotional well-being of their teams, organizations can create a more resilient workforce that is better equipped to handle challenges and thrive in today's fast-paced business environment.

As you promote a healthier work environment within your team, it's essential to focus on practical strategies that can be easily implemented. Encouraging open communication is a key aspect of fostering a positive workplace atmosphere. By creating a space where team members feel comfortable sharing their thoughts, concerns, and ideas, you can build trust and strengthen relationships within the team.

Another effective strategy is to recognize and celebrate achievements regularly. Acknowledging team members' hard work and contributions boosts morale and reinforces a sense of value and appreciation. Consider implementing a recognition program that highlights individual and team accomplishments, fostering a culture of positivity and encouragement.

Setting clear goals and expectations is crucial for promoting a healthy work environment. When team members clearly understand what is expected of them and how their contributions align with the team's objectives, they are more likely to feel motivated and engaged. Regularly communicate goals, provide feedback on progress, and adjust expectations as needed to ensure everyone is on the same page.

Promoting work-life balance is also vital for creating a healthy workplace culture. Encourage team members to prioritize self-care, take breaks when needed, and disconnect from work outside office hours. By supporting well-being inside and outside the workplace, you can help prevent burnout and maintain high levels of job satisfaction among your team.

Regular team-building activities can further strengthen relationships among team members and improve collaboration. These activities allow team members to interact more relaxedly, fostering camaraderie and trust. Consider organizing virtual or in-person events that cater to different interests and preferences within the team.

Creating a supportive feedback culture is essential for promoting growth and development within the team.

Encourage constructive feedback exchanges among team members, focusing on areas for improvement and strengths. By fostering a culture where feedback is seen as a tool for growth rather than criticism, you can empower your team to continuously learn and evolve.

Lastly, lead by example when promoting a healthier work environment. Demonstrate behaviors such as active listening, empathy, transparency, and resilience in your interactions with the team. Your actions will set the tone for the workplace culture and inspire others to create a positive and supportive environment for all team members.

The Power of Team Synergy

Team building is more than just an opportunity for fun and games; it's vital to fostering a supportive, stress-free workplace. Through carefully designed activities, we enhance team collaboration and significantly boost each member's psychological and emotional well-being. This ripple effect of positive emotions leads to improved morale, which is crucial in today's high-pressure work environments.

Understanding the deep-seated emotional benefits of these activities helps us see that their value extends far beyond the surface. They are critical tools for reducing workplace stress enabling individuals to perform at their best. Integrating strategic team-building exercises lays the groundwork for a more harmonious and efficient work setting.

Applying these strategies is not merely a suggestion but necessary for cultivating a healthier work environment. It's about taking proactive steps to ensure every team member feels valued, understood, and connected to their peers. This sense of belonging ultimately drives a team's overall efficiency and success.

Let's empower ourselves and our teams by embracing these practices. Doing so enhances our immediate work atmosphere and contributes to a more vibrant, productive, and satisfying organizational culture. Remember, when a team feels good together, it performs exceptionally well together. Let this understanding guide us as we continue to develop and strengthen our teams, ensuring that every member feels supported and motivated to contribute their best.

Embrace these insights and strategies confidently, knowing they are designed to foster a better work environment and a more fulfilling professional life for everyone involved.

Chapter 13: Evolution of Team Dynamics

> "The greatest weapon against stress
>
> is our ability to choose one
>
> thought over another."
>
> **William James**

Is Your Team Building Strategy Evolving as Fast as Your Team?

The static, once-a-year team building retreat is no longer sufficient in today's rapidly changing work environment. As teams become more diverse and projects more dynamic, the traditional approaches to team building can quickly become outdated. The need for continuous evaluation and improvement in team-building strategies has never been more critical. This necessity forms the backbone of our discussion on keeping team dynamics fluid and effective, ensuring that every member feels engaged and aligned with the broader organizational goals.

The Imperative of Continuous Improvement

Continuous improvement isn't just a buzzword; it's a vital practice that can determine the success or failure of team synergy. Teams are living entities that evolve, with new challenges and opportunities emerging at every turn. Without regular assessment and updates to team-building activities, there's a real risk of these initiatives becoming stale or irrelevant. This can lead to disengagement and a drop in productivity, which no organization can afford in today's competitive landscape.

Strategies for Regular Assessment

To avoid this pitfall, it is essential to develop methods for regular assessment of team dynamics. This does not merely involve occasional feedback sessions but requires a structured approach to understanding how team interactions develop over time and how they can be enhanced. This proactive stance helps pinpoint areas where the team excels and needs more support, allowing leaders to tailor their strategies effectively.

Cultivating a Culture of Professional Development

Moreover, integrating team building into ongoing professional development can yield significant benefits. It encourages a culture where continuous learning and collaboration are valued, enhancing team performance. By making team building part of everyday processes rather than a yearly event, organizations can ensure that their teams are always at the peak of their collaborative potential.

Keeping Activities Fresh and Aligned

Maintaining an effective team-building strategy keeps the activities fresh and closely aligned with organizational goals. This alignment ensures that each exercise or initiative is fun and enriches the participants' professional skills and understanding of the company's objectives. It transforms standard activities into powerful tools for personal growth and organizational development.

Responding to Evolving Team Dynamics

Teams change—new members join, others leave, company goals shift, and external pressures vary. Each change affects the dynamics within the group, necessitating adjustments to how we approach team building. Recognizing this fluidity and preparing to adapt accordingly is crucial for maintaining an environment where all members feel valued and understood.

Organizations can better support their teams in achieving outstanding results by fostering an atmosphere that prioritizes regular evaluation and refinement of team-building activities. This approach not only boosts morale but also drives innovation by ensuring that every member has an opportunity to contribute to their fullest potential.

By embracing these principles, organizations can create a vibrant culture of continuous improvement that propels teams toward achieving exceptional performance levels while remaining agile in a fast-paced world.

Continuous evaluation and improvement in team-building strategies are vital for the sustained success of any team. As teams evolve, so do their dynamics, requiring a proactive approach to ensure that team-building activities remain effective and relevant. Regular assessment and refinement of these activities help keep them engaging, aligned with organizational goals, and responsive to the changing needs of the team members.

To maintain the benefits of team-building initiatives, it is crucial to continuously evaluate their impact on the team's performance and cohesion. By collecting feedback from team members, leaders can identify areas needing improvement and tailor future activities to address these needs. This feedback loop fosters a culture of open communication and collaboration within the team, enhancing trust and mutual understanding among members.

Incorporating feedback into the design of team-building activities allows for a more personalized approach that resonates with the unique characteristics of the team. By customizing activities based on feedback, leaders can create more meaningful experiences that cater to team members' diverse preferences and working styles. This tailored approach increases engagement and ensures that the activities are relevant and impactful for all participants.

Regular assessment of team building strategies is essential to gauge their effectiveness over time. By tracking key performance indicators related to teamwork, communication, and productivity, leaders can measure these activities' impact on the team's overall performance. This data-driven approach provides valuable insights into areas of strength and improvement, guiding future decisions on team-building initiatives.

Refinement of team building activities based on assessment results is key to ensuring continuous growth and development within the team. By analyzing feedback and performance data, leaders can identify patterns and trends that inform adjustments to existing activities or the introduction of new ones. This iterative process allows for ongoing improvement and innovation in team-building strategies, keeping them fresh, relevant, and impactful.

Continuous Assessment and Refinement of Team Building Activities

Continuous assessment and refinement of team-building activities are crucial for maintaining a high level of effectiveness within a team. Regular evaluation allows leaders to identify what is working well and what may need adjustment, ensuring that team-building strategies remain relevant and impactful. By implementing methods for assessing the outcomes of team-building activities, leaders can gather valuable feedback from team members, analyze the results, and make informed decisions on how to refine future initiatives.

One effective method for regular assessment is through feedback sessions. Encouraging team members to share their thoughts, experiences, and suggestions after each team-building activity can provide valuable insights into what aspects were successful and what areas may require improvement. Open communication channels within the team foster a culture of transparency and collaboration, enabling continuous growth and development.

Self-assessment tools can also be valuable resources for teams evaluating their dynamics objectively. Utilizing surveys, questionnaires, or assessments designed to measure teamwork, communication, and trust levels can offer quantitative data on the effectiveness of team-building efforts. These tools provide concrete feedback that can guide leaders in making informed decisions on adjusting their strategies.

In addition to regular assessments, ongoing refinement of team-building activities is essential for keeping them engaging and aligned with the team's evolving needs. Leaders should be open to experimenting with new approaches and adapting existing activities based on feedback received. Flexibility and willingness to evolve are key traits of successful teams continuously striving for improvement.

Another effective strategy for refining team-building activities is incorporating variety into the initiatives. Introducing new challenges, themes, or formats can help maintain team engagement and prevent activities from becoming monotonous or predictable. Creativity and innovation in designing team-building exercises can spark excitement among team members and promote a culture of continuous learning and growth.

Moreover, regular reflection sessions following team building activities can allow teams to collectively analyze their experiences, celebrate successes, and identify areas for improvement. Reflective discussions allow team members to share perspectives, insights, and lessons learned, fostering a deeper understanding of each other's strengths and weaknesses.

By developing regular assessment and refinement methods of team building activities, leaders can ensure that their efforts contribute effectively to enhancing teamwork, communication, and collaboration within the team. Embracing a continuous improvement mindset fosters a culture of adaptability, creativity, and resilience that propels teams toward peak performance in today's dynamic work environments.

In cultivating a culture of ongoing professional development and team building maintenance, it is essential to prioritize consistent efforts toward nurturing team dynamics. Encouraging a continuous learning mindset within the team can foster growth and adaptability. Team members can stay engaged and motivated by providing opportunities for skill development and knowledge enhancement. Regular training sessions, workshops, and seminars can be instrumental in keeping the team updated with the latest trends and practices in their field.

Empowering team members to take ownership of their professional growth is key to fostering a culture of ongoing development. Encouraging them to set personal goals and offering support to achieve these objectives can increase job satisfaction and productivity. Creating a supportive environment where individuals feel valued for their contributions and have room for growth can significantly impact team cohesion.

Regular feedback sessions are crucial to maintaining effective team building. Providing constructive feedback on individual and team performance can help identify areas for improvement and recognize achievements. Open communication channels within the team facilitate discussions about challenges, successes, and ways to enhance collaboration.

Implementing team-building activities at regular intervals can inject energy into the group dynamic. These activities range from fun icebreakers to more structured problem-solving exercises promoting teamwork and creativity. Tailoring activities to address specific team needs or challenges can make them more impactful and relevant.

Encouraging a culture of ongoing professional development also involves recognizing individual strengths within the team. By leveraging these strengths, teams can work more efficiently towards common goals. Assigning tasks based on expertise and providing opportunities for skill-sharing can enhance collaboration and build trust among team members.

As we navigate the complexities of team dynamics, it becomes clear that the journey toward optimal performance is continuous and ever-evolving. The necessity for regular evaluation and enhancement of team-building strategies cannot be overstated. By committing to this ongoing process, organizations ensure that their teams meet current standards and are poised for future challenges and opportunities.

Implementing methods for regular assessment and refinement of activities serves as a cornerstone for this continuous improvement. It empowers teams to remain relevant and effective, adapting to both internal growth and external changes. This adaptability is crucial in maintaining engagement and productivity within diverse work environments, in-person or virtual.

Furthermore, fostering a culture of ongoing professional development and maintenance of team building ensures that these efforts are sustainable. It underscores the importance of investing in human capital and the long-term benefits of such investments. Teams that embrace this culture are better equipped to handle the demands of modern workspaces and can leverage their collective skills more effectively.

Through these practices, organizations can achieve a harmonious balance between meeting immediate goals and nurturing long-term development. This approach not only enhances the performance of teams but also contributes to a more dynamic and resilient organizational culture.

By actively engaging in these strategies, you are taking a significant step towards creating an environment where continuous growth is encouraged and integrated into the fabric of your team's operations. Remember, the strength of a team lies not just in the skills of its members but in how effectively they are harnessed and developed over time. Embrace this journey confidently, knowing each step is a building block for sustained success.

Chapter 14: The Future of Team Synergy

"Adaptability is about the powerful difference between adapting to cope and adapting to win."

Max McKeown

Embracing Tomorrow: How New Technologies Are Redefining Team Building

As we navigate the evolving landscape of workplace dynamics, the advent of groundbreaking technologies promises a transformative leap in how teams collaborate and thrive. This pivotal moment in team development is not just about adopting new tools; it's about reimagining the potential of collective effort to achieve unparalleled results. Integrating virtual reality (VR) and artificial intelligence (AI) into team-building exercises presents an exciting frontier for leaders eager to enhance team synergy and performance.

Emerging technologies are reshaping the terrain of professional teamwork, making it imperative for leaders to stay abreast of these changes to foster an environment where innovation flourishes. As we explore these modern tools, it becomes clear that they offer more than just novel experiences; they provide dynamic pathways to deepen engagement and understanding among team members. By leveraging VR, teams can simulate complex, collaborative scenarios that would be costly or impossible to recreate in real life. At the same time, AI-driven simulations can predict team dynamics and provide insights into improving collaboration.

The potential of these technologies extends beyond simple task execution; they are pivotal in crafting an immersive learning environment that mirrors real-world challenges. This approach enhances problem-solving skills and bolsters emotional connections as team members navigate shared virtual experiences. The emotional resonance created through such engagements is invaluable in building trust and empathy, which are the cornerstones of a robust team dynamic.

Integrating these innovations into existing team building frameworks involves a strategic understanding of their capabilities and limitations. It is essential for leaders to not only equip themselves with these tools but also to cultivate an adaptive mindset among their teams. This readiness to embrace change will enable organizations to effectively leverage technological advancements.

In synthesizing the main themes explored throughout this book, it becomes evident that effective team building is not static but an evolving practice that must adapt to the shifting paradigms of work environments, including remote and hybrid models. The insights from traditional exercises and cutting-edge technology-driven approaches provide a comprehensive toolkit for enhancing team performance.

The journey through various team-building exercises discussed in this book culminates here—where tradition meets innovation. By understanding and applying these insights, leaders are well-equipped to foster an atmosphere of continuous improvement and high performance. Embracing these new methodologies will propel teams towards operational excellence and ensure a resilient and adaptive organizational culture ready to face future challenges.

In essence, as we look toward the future of team synergy, it is clear that our approach must be as dynamic as the technologies we seek to integrate. This chapter sets the stage for a deeper exploration into how these technological advancements can be seamlessly woven into effective team-building strategies, ensuring sustained success in a rapidly changing world.

Emerging technologies are reshaping the landscape of team building, offering exciting new avenues for enhancing synergy among team members. Virtual reality (VR) exercises and AI-driven simulations are revolutionizing traditional team-building methods, providing immersive experiences that can bridge physical distances and foster collaboration in unprecedented ways. By leveraging these cutting-edge tools, teams can transcend conventional boundaries and tap into a realm of interactive possibilities that were once unimaginable.

With its ability to create lifelike environments and scenarios, virtual reality allows team members to engage in realistic simulations that mimic real-world challenges. Through VR team-building exercises, individuals can work together to solve complex problems, communicate effectively, and build trust in a dynamic and interactive setting. This technology offers a unique opportunity for teams to practice decision-making under pressure, enhance problem-solving skills, and strengthen interpersonal relationships in a safe yet engaging environment.

On the other hand, AI-driven simulations bring a new level of sophistication to team-building activities by providing personalized feedback and insights based on individual performance. These simulations can adapt to the needs of each team member, offering tailored guidance and support to help individuals improve their communication, leadership, and collaboration skills. By harnessing the power of artificial intelligence, teams can benefit from data-driven insights that facilitate continuous growth and development among team members.

As organizations embrace these innovative technologies, they open up possibilities for enhancing team engagement and fostering a culture of continuous improvement. Virtual reality experiences can inject excitement and novelty into team-building activities, capturing the interest and enthusiasm of participants in a way that traditional methods may struggle to achieve. Similarly, AI-driven simulations offer a personalized approach to skill development, empowering team members to take ownership of their growth and progress within the team dynamic.

By staying abreast of these emerging team-building trends, leaders can position their teams at the forefront of innovation and prepare for the future of collaborative work environments. As technology evolves rapidly, teams must adapt and embrace new tools to drive performance and efficiency. Virtual reality exercises and AI-driven simulations represent just the beginning of a wave of technological advancements that promise to revolutionize how teams interact, communicate, and collaborate in the coming years.

Embracing Innovative Tools for Enhancing Team Engagement and Synergy

As team dynamics continue to evolve, it is crucial to explore how new tools can enhance team engagement and synergy. In today's rapidly changing work environment, staying abreast of technological advancements can give teams the edge they need to excel. Incorporating innovative tools and strategies can boost collaboration, communication, and overall productivity within a team setting.

One key tool that can significantly enhance team engagement is virtual reality (VR). VR simulations offer a unique and immersive experience that allows team members to interact in a virtual environment. This technology can particularly benefit remote teams or those spread across different locations. By simulating real-life scenarios, team members can develop problem-solving skills, enhance decision-making, and improve overall communication within a safe and controlled setting.

Another valuable tool for enhancing team synergy is AI-driven simulations. These simulations use artificial intelligence to create scenarios that mimic real-world challenges. By engaging in these simulations, team members can practice working together effectively, learn how to adapt to various situations, and strengthen their problem-solving skills. AI-driven simulations provide a dynamic and interactive way for teams to hone their collaboration skills and build stronger relationships.

Utilizing project management software can also foster team engagement and synergy. Platforms like Trello, Asana, or Monday.com offer features that streamline task assignments, progress tracking, and communication within a team. These tools can enhance efficiency and promote unity among team members by centralizing project information and facilitating seamless collaboration.

Video conferencing tools like Zoom or Microsoft Teams can improve team engagement, especially for remote or hybrid teams. Video calls allow face-to-face interaction, fostering better communication and understanding among team members. Regular video meetings can help build rapport, strengthen relationships, and create a more cohesive team dynamic.

Gamification is another innovative approach that can boost team engagement and synergy. Teams can feel more motivated and connected by introducing game elements into tasks or projects, such as point systems, rewards, or friendly competition. Gamification encourages active participation, fosters teamwork, and injects fun into daily work activities.

Encouraging open communication channels through messaging apps like Slack or Microsoft Teams fosters real-time collaboration, enabling team members to instantly share ideas, ask questions, and provide feedback. These platforms facilitate quick decision-making processes and create a more transparent work environment where everyone's voice is heard.

Implementing feedback tools like 360-degree assessments or pulse surveys allows teams to gather valuable insights, identify improvement areas, and address issues proactively. Regular feedback sessions promote continuous growth and development within the team, leading to enhanced performance and increased synergy among members.

Organizations can cultivate a more collaborative, efficient, and cohesive work environment by leveraging these new tools and approaches to enhance team engagement and synergy. Embracing innovation in team building boosts productivity and fosters a sense of camaraderie and shared purpose among team members.

As you prepare to integrate future innovations into your current team-building practices, staying informed about the latest trends and technologies shaping the landscape of team synergy is essential. Embracing change and being open to new methods can significantly enhance your team's dynamics and overall performance. By proactively seeking out innovative approaches, you position yourself as a forward-thinker in team development, ready to adapt to the evolving needs of your team members.

Stay Curious and Explore: Keep an open mind towards emerging technologies and trends in team building. Actively seek information on virtual reality exercises, AI-driven simulations, or other cutting-edge tools that can revolutionize how teams interact and collaborate. Being curious and exploring new possibilities will enable you to discover novel ways to engage your team members effectively.

Embrace Flexibility: Flexibility is key in the fast-paced world of modern work environments. As you prepare to integrate future innovations into your team-building practices, be prepared to adapt and adjust your strategies based on the unique needs of your team. Flexibility allows you to tailor your approach to different situations and individuals, fostering a more inclusive and dynamic team environment.

Encourage Experimentation: Don't be afraid to experiment with new tools and techniques in your team-building efforts. Encouraging experimentation fosters a culture of innovation within your team, where members feel empowered to explore unconventional methods and solutions. By embracing a spirit of experimentation, you create space for creativity and growth, leading to breakthroughs in team synergy.

Seek Feedback and Iterate: As you incorporate new innovations into your team-building practices, seek feedback from team members on their experiences. Use this feedback to iterate your approaches, refining them based on real-world insights and suggestions. You demonstrate a commitment to continuous improvement and optimization by actively involving your team in the process.

Create a Roadmap for Implementation: Develop a clear roadmap for integrating future innovations into your team-building practices. Outline specific goals, timelines, and milestones to track progress effectively. Having a structured plan ensures that you stay focused on your objectives and can measure the impact of new initiatives on your team's synergy.

Foster a Culture of Lifelong Learning: Encourage lifelong learning within your team, where members are eager to explore new ideas and acquire new skills. Provide opportunities for professional development and training related to emerging technologies in team building. By fostering a growth mindset among your team members, you lay the foundation for continuous innovation and improvement.

Celebrate Successes and Learn from Failures: Celebrate successes that result from integrating future innovations into your team-building practices. Acknowledge achievements, both big and small, reinforcing positive behaviors within your team. Additionally, failures should be viewed as learning opportunities rather than setbacks, extracting valuable insights to inform future strategies. By embracing a culture of celebration and learning, you create a resilient and adaptive team ready to tackle any challenge that comes their way.

As you prepare to embrace the future of team synergy through innovative technologies and trends, remember that change is constant in today's dynamic work environment. By staying proactive, flexible, and open-minded, you can lead your team toward peak performance by leveraging the power of new tools and approaches in team building.

Emerging technologies and trends are rapidly transforming the landscape of team building. Virtual reality, AI-driven simulations, and other innovative tools offer unprecedented opportunities to engage and unify teams in ways that were unimaginable just a few years ago. Embracing these technologies can significantly enhance team synergy and performance, making it crucial for leaders and managers to stay informed and adaptable.

Integrating these new tools into team-building practices is about keeping up with technology and seizing opportunities to foster a deeper connection and understanding among team members. Whether through immersive virtual environments or sophisticated simulations that predict team dynamics, these technologies enable a more engaging and effective team-building experience.

Practical implementation of these innovations requires a thoughtful approach. It involves understanding your team's specific needs and dynamics, choosing the right technologies, and customizing exercises that leverage these tools effectively. The goal is to enhance communication, trust, and collaboration among team members, bridging gaps that physical distances or cultural differences might create.

Throughout this book, we have explored a variety of exercises and strategies designed to improve team performance. From traditional activities to cutting-edge virtual solutions, the overarching theme has been clear: effective team building is essential for achieving and sustaining peak performance in any organization. Applying the insights and strategies discussed can transform your team's dynamics, fostering a more cohesive, motivated, and high-performing environment.

As we progress, the challenge for every team leader and manager is to remain flexible and innovative. Embrace the continuous evolution of technology as part of your strategy to enhance team synergy. Encourage ongoing learning and adaptation among your team members. The future of team building is dynamic and promising, filled with potential for those willing to explore and implement these new approaches.

The journey to achieving peak team performance is ongoing and ever-evolving. By staying proactive and informed about emerging technologies and trends in team building, you can ensure your team adapts and thrives in the changing landscape of work environments. Remember, the strength of your team lies in its ability to grow together—leveraging new tools and technologies is just one of many steps in this continuous development path.

Epilogue

"Life is a series of natural and spontaneous changes. Don't resist them; that only creates sorrow."

Lao Tzu

Embracing the Future: A Journey Towards Exceptional Team Synergy

As we draw this guide to a close, we must reflect on the journey we've embarked upon together. From understanding the foundational elements of team dynamics to applying innovative exercises tailored for in-person and virtual environments, this book has aimed to equip you with the tools necessary to transform your team into a high-performing powerhouse.

The real-world applications of the strategies discussed are vast and varied. Whether leading a small startup or managing a department within a large corporation, effective team-building and management principles are universally applicable. Implementing these exercises can lead to improved communication, increased productivity, and a workplace atmosphere that is both inclusive and motivating.

We've covered essential topics such as fostering trust, enhancing communication, and adapting to diverse team needs in different settings. Key takeaways include the importance of regular and open communication, trust and mutual respect among team members, and the need for continuous adaptation to technological advancements and cultural shifts within teams.

To implement these insights, start by assessing your current team dynamics and identifying areas that require improvement. Implement the suggested exercises gradually, ensuring that feedback from team members is gathered and adjustments made as necessary. Remember, the goal is to enhance productivity and foster an environment where every team member feels valued and understood.

While this book provides comprehensive guidance, it's important to acknowledge that team dynamics continually evolve. Further research might explore deeper psychological aspects of team interactions or emerging digital tools facilitating remote collaboration. Always stay curious and open to new ideas that could further enhance your team's cohesion and performance.

Now is the time for action. Use what you've learned here to improve your team's performance and contribute positively to their professional growth and personal satisfaction. Empower them with confidence, equip them with skills, and lead by example.

Let's conclude with a thought-provoking quote that encapsulates our discussions:

"Coming together is a beginning; keeping together is progress; working together is success."

Henry Ford

This timeless piece of wisdom reminds us that while forming a team is the initial step, the true achievement lies in nurturing that group into a cohesive unit that achieves collective success through shared efforts and mutual support.

May your journey in leading and nurturing your teams be as rewarding as successful!

Conclusion

"The art of life lies in a constant readjustment to our surroundings."

Kakuzo Okakura

Building and nurturing high-performing teams is an ongoing journey that requires dedication, adaptability, and a commitment to continuous improvement. Throughout this guide, we have explored myriad strategies and techniques designed to enhance teamwork, whether in physical spaces or through virtual means. The insights shared here aim to equip you with the skills needed to foster an environment where your team can thrive, no matter the challenges that lie ahead.

Trust, communication, and adaptability are the bedrock of effective teamwork. By prioritizing these elements, you ensure a solid foundation for your team to build and excel. Encouraging open communication, fostering mutual respect, and demonstrating flexibility in the face of change are crucial to creating a cohesive and dynamic team.

As a leader or team member committed to excellence, embracing continuous learning and development is imperative. The techniques and strategies outlined in this guide are not static; they require regular reassessment and refinement in response to evolving circumstances and emerging technologies. By maintaining a mindset of perpetual growth, you can inspire your team to do the same, resulting in sustained high performance and innovation.

Integrating traditional methods with new technological solutions is another key aspect of this guide. By balancing time-tested team-building activities with cutting-edge digital tools, you can create a versatile and engaging experience for your team. This hybrid approach ensures that your team remains agile and capable of navigating the complexities of modern work environments, whether operating remotely, in-person, or through a hybrid model.

This guide has provided concrete steps for assessing and improving your team's dynamics to facilitate practical application. Implementing these steps allows you to identify areas of strength and opportunities for growth, enabling you to make informed adjustments that enhance overall performance. The goal is to create a sustainable development model that yields measurable, long-term benefits for your team.

To summarise the key takeaways:

- Prioritise trust and mutual respect within your team.
- Enhance communication skills through practical exercises and digital tools.

- Embrace adaptability and remain flexible in diverse work environments.
- Foster a culture of continuous learning and development.
- Integrate traditional team-building methods with modern technological solutions.
- Regularly assess and refine your team-building strategies for sustained success.

By adhering to these principles and strategies, you can lead your team with confidence and competence. Remember that effective teamwork is not a destination but a continuous journey that requires vigilance, innovation, and an ever-present willingness to adapt and learn.

As you move forward, let this guide serve as both a foundation and a springboard for your efforts in team-building. The ultimate power of a team lies in its ability to grow together, leveraging individual strengths toward a common goal. With the tools and insights provided here, you can create an environment where every team member feels valued and empowered to contribute to collective success.

May your endeavors to foster exceptional teamwork be fruitful, rewarding, and marked by the enduring success of your team and your leadership.

Bonus Material

Your Questions, Answered!

1. How Can I Effectively Measure the Success of the New Team-Building Strategies Implemented?

Effectively measuring the success of new team-building strategies involves a multi-faceted approach that blends qualitative and quantitative metrics. A key starting point is establishing measurable goals tailored to your team's unique dynamics and organizational objectives. These goals might include improved communication, increased productivity, enhanced collaboration, or higher morale. Once defined, these objectives should be communicated transparently with all team members to ensure collective understanding and alignment.

To gather quantitative data, consider implementing regular surveys and feedback forms that assess various aspects of team performance and satisfaction. Tools like Net Promoter Score (NPS) can provide insights into team sentiment and willingness to collaborate. Additionally, tracking specific performance metrics such as project completion rates, error rates, and meeting participation levels can offer concrete evidence of progress or areas needing improvement. Regularly review these metrics to identify trends and assess the impact of the team-building strategies over time.

Qualitative feedback is equally important for a comprehensive evaluation. Conduct one-on-one interviews or small group discussions to delve deeper into individual experiences and perceptions. This approach allows team members to voice concerns or highlight successes that might not be apparent in quantitative data. Creating a safe and open environment for these conversations is crucial, as it encourages honest and constructive feedback. This qualitative insight can be particularly valuable for understanding the nuances of team dynamics and for identifying less tangible improvements in areas such as trust and cohesion.

Another critical aspect of measuring team-building strategies' success is fostering a culture of continuous feedback and reflection. Regularly scheduled retrospectives or review meetings can serve as platforms for the team to collectively assess what is working well and what may need adjustment. Encouraging a growth mindset where feedback is seen as an opportunity for improvement can help sustain momentum and ensure that strategies remain effective and relevant.

Lastly, consider integrating technology to support and streamline the measurement process. Tools such as project management software, virtual collaboration platforms, and performance analytics can provide real-time data and insights. These technologies allow for more agile responses and timely adjustments to your team-building efforts. By combining traditional methods and modern technologies, you can create a robust framework for evaluating the success of your team-building strategies, ultimately leading to a more cohesive and high-performing team.

2. What Are Some Common Obstacles I Might Face When Trying to Foster a Culture of Continuous Improvement, and How Can I Overcome Them?

Fostering a culture of continuous improvement is essential for maintaining a dynamic and progressive team environment. However, this ambitious endeavor often encounters several common obstacles that can hinder its success. One significant challenge is resistance to change. Employees may feel comfortable with established routines and processes and be apprehensive about adopting new methods or adapting to evolving expectations. To address this, clearly communicating the benefits of continuous improvement clearly is crucial. Regularly highlight success stories where change has led to positive outcomes and ensure that team members understand how these transformations contribute to personal and collective growth.

Another critical obstacle is a lack of resources, including time, training, or financial investment. Continuous improvement requires dedicated effort and sometimes adjustments in resource allocation. An effective strategy to overcome this hurdle is to integrate improvement initiatives into the daily workflow.

Encourage incremental changes that can be managed within existing structures and provide ongoing training and development opportunities to build the necessary skills. Leadership support is also vital; demonstrating commitment through resource allocation and active participation sets a powerful example for the team.

Communication barriers can also impede continuous improvement. When feedback and ideas are not freely exchanged, it stifles innovation and prevents the identification of growth opportunities. To counteract this, create an open and transparent communication culture where team members feel safe to share their thoughts and suggestions. Regular feedback loops, anonymous suggestion boxes, and open forums or town hall meetings can facilitate this flow of information. By prioritizing open dialogue, you enable the exchange of diverse perspectives, fostering a richer environment for continuous improvement.

Lastly, sustaining momentum over the long term can be challenging. Initial enthusiasm for improvement projects may wane as daily pressures and setbacks arise. To maintain momentum, celebrate small wins, and recognize the efforts of individuals and teams contributing to continuous improvement. Implement regular review processes to assess progress and identify areas for further development. Additionally, embedding continuous improvement into the organization's values and mission ensures it remains a core focus rather than a temporary initiative. By addressing these obstacles with thoughtful and strategic approaches, you can build and sustain a culture of continuous improvement that propels your team and organization forward.

3. How Do I Encourage Team Members to Provide Honest and Constructive Feedback?

Encouraging team members to provide honest and constructive feedback is crucial for fostering a culture of continuous improvement. One effective way to achieve this is by establishing a safe and supportive environment where feedback is valued and respected. Leaders play a pivotal role in setting the tone for open communication. By demonstrating vulnerability and openness, leaders can create a space where team members feel comfortable sharing their thoughts and experiences without fear of retaliation or judgment. Regularly emphasizing the importance of feedback in team meetings and individual conversations can reinforce its value and encourage active participation.

Another strategy is implementing structured feedback mechanisms that provide clear guidelines for delivering constructive feedback. Training sessions and workshops on effective communication can equip team members with the necessary skills to articulate their perspectives thoughtfully and respectfully. Additionally, adopting specific frameworks, such as the "Situation-Behavior-Impact" (SBI) model, can help standardize the feedback process and ensure that comments are actionable and focused on behaviors rather than personal attributes. This structured approach makes it easier for members to give feedback and ensures that the feedback received is relevant and productive.

Creating opportunities for regular feedback exchange is also essential. Implementing routine feedback sessions, such as one-on-one meetings, peer reviews, or team retrospectives, can normalize the practice and make it an integral part of the team's workflow. During these sessions, encourage team members to share positive and constructive feedback, fostering a balanced view of performance and promoting a growth mindset. It's also beneficial to provide anonymous feedback channels to protect the identities of those who may have reservations about speaking up directly. This anonymity can help in surfacing critical insights that might otherwise be suppressed.

Finally, it is vital to act on the feedback received. When team members see that their input leads to tangible changes or improvements, it validates their contributions and motivates them to continue participating in the feedback process. Acknowledge the feedback publicly, outline the steps that will be taken to address the concerns raised, and follow through with those actions. This accountability enhances trust within the team and demonstrates that feedback is taken seriously and can drive positive change. By implementing these strategies, you can cultivate an environment where honest and constructive feedback thrives, ultimately enhancing team performance and satisfaction.

4. What Specific Digital Tools Can Be Best Integrated With Traditional Team-Building Methods?

In today's hybrid work environment, integrating digital tools with traditional team-building methods can significantly enhance team cohesion, productivity, and morale. Digital tools offer flexibility and accessibility, allowing teams to collaborate and bond regardless of geographic location. The first step in integration involves choosing the right digital platforms that complement traditional methods. Video conferencing tools like Zoom and Microsoft Teams enable face-to-face interactions, which is essential for building rapport and trust within a team. These platforms can host virtual team-building activities such as trivia games, workshops, and even virtual escape rooms, which mirror traditional team-building exercises online.

Project management tools like Trello, Asana, or Monday.com can be integrated into team-building by making collaborative tasks transparent and manageable. These tools allow team members to track progress, assign tasks, and communicate efficiently, fostering a sense of shared responsibility and unity. Regular virtual check-ins and progress updates can also be designed as team-building exercises, where team members reflect on their achievements and highlight areas of improvement collaboratively. This encourages a continuous feedback loop and promotes a collective growth and learning culture, which traditional methods aim to achieve.

Furthermore, digital platforms designed for team engagement, like Slack or Microsoft Teams, offer various plugins and integrations that host virtual lounges or breakout rooms for informal interactions. These "digital watercoolers" can be used for casual conversations, brainstorming sessions, or even virtual coffee breaks, mirroring the social aspects of traditional office environments. Incorporating these casual meetups can relieve workplace stress and strengthen interpersonal relationships, similar to traditional team-building outings or offsite retreats.

Lastly, leveraging digital tools for real-time recognition and rewards can enhance traditional team-building efforts. Platforms like Bonusly or Kudos allow team members to give and receive recognition instantly, celebrating achievements and reinforcing positive behaviors. This boosts morale and aligns with the traditional team-building approach of acknowledging and appreciating individual and team efforts. Incorporating digital tools effectively bridges the gap between remote and in-person interactions, ensuring that the essence of team-building remains intact while adapting to the evolving work landscape.

5. How Can I Adapt Team-Building Strategies to Suit Remote or Hybrid Work Environments?

Adapting team-building strategies to suit remote or hybrid work environments requires a thoughtful approach considering the unique challenges and opportunities presented by these setups.

A primary step in this adaptation process is to ensure that team-building activities are inclusive and accessible to all team members, regardless of their location. This may involve utilizing digital tools and platforms that facilitate virtual interaction, such as video conferencing software, collaboration tools, and social engagement apps. For instance, virtual team-building exercises like online trivia games, virtual escape rooms, or remote workshops can mirror in-person activities' interactive and collaborative nature while accommodating the remote setting.

Maintaining regular and structured communication is another critical aspect of adapting team-building strategies for remote or hybrid work environments. Establishing clear communication channels and scheduling regular check-ins can help keep team members connected and engaged. Virtual one-on-one meetings, team meetings, and informal catch-ups can serve the same purpose as traditional office interactions, fostering a sense of belonging and camaraderie. Additionally, implementing digital project management tools such as Trello, Asana, or Monday.com can help streamline collaboration, track progress, and ensure everyone stays aligned with shared goals and responsibilities.

Building a strong team culture in a remote or hybrid environment also involves creating opportunities for social interaction and relationship-building outside formal work contexts. Virtual "water cooler" moments, such as casual chat rooms, virtual coffee breaks, or online social events, can help replicate the spontaneous and informal interactions in physical office spaces. These informal touchpoints are essential for developing trust and rapport among team members, foundational elements of effective team-building.

Furthermore, recognizing and celebrating achievements in a remote or hybrid work environment can reinforce positive behaviors and boost morale. Digital recognition platforms like Bonusly or Kudos enable team members to give and receive instant recognition, making it easier to celebrate successes and appreciate contributions in real-time. Regular recognition and reward mechanisms motivate individuals and strengthen the overall team dynamic, making everyone feel valued and appreciated.

In conclusion, adapting team-building strategies to suit remote or hybrid work environments requires leveraging digital tools and platforms, maintaining regular communication, fostering social interactions, and recognizing achievements. By thoughtfully designing team-building activities that accommodate remote settings, organizations can ensure that their teams remain cohesive, engaged, and productive, regardless of physical location. This adapted approach can help bridge the gap between remote and in-person interactions, ensuring that the core objectives of team-building are met in an evolving work landscape.

6. How Can I Address Trust and Mutual Respect Issues When Existing Conflicts Are Present Within the Team?

Addressing issues of trust and mutual respect within a team, especially when existing conflicts are present, requires a multifaceted approach rooted in open communication, empathy, and structured conflict resolution mechanisms. First and foremost, creating a safe and inclusive environment where team members feel comfortable expressing their concerns and grievances is essential. This can be facilitated through regular team meetings dedicated to discussing interpersonal dynamics and one-on-one sessions where individuals can voice their feelings without fear of retribution. Establishing a culture of transparency can help identify underlying issues and prevent them from festering into more significant conflicts.

Empathy plays a crucial role in resolving conflicts and rebuilding trust. Encouraging team members to actively listen to one another and understand different perspectives can foster a sense of mutual respect and facilitate the healing process. Leadership can lead by example by demonstrating empathy in their interactions and acknowledging the emotional and psychological dimensions underlying many workplace conflicts. This empathetic approach can help humanize the conflict and make it easier for team members to find common ground and work towards resolution.

Implementing structured conflict resolution mechanisms is another vital step in addressing trust and mutual respect issues. Developing clear policies and procedures for conflict resolution and ensuring all team members know them can provide a consistent framework for addressing disputes. Utilizing mediation or involving a neutral third party can also be beneficial when conflicts are particularly entrenched or complex. These structures can help objectively assess conflicts and devise fair and equitable solutions that consider the interests of all parties involved.

Finally, fostering a culture of continuous feedback and improvement is essential for maintaining trust and respect over the long term. Regularly revisiting team dynamics through performance reviews, feedback sessions, and team-building exercises can help identify potential issues before they escalate. Celebrating small wins and recognizing efforts to resolve conflicts can reinforce positive behavior and contribute to a more cohesive and harmonious team environment.

By incorporating open communication, empathy, structured conflict resolution, and continuous feedback, organizations can effectively address issues of trust and mutual respect even when existing conflicts exist. These strategies help resolve current disputes and lay the groundwork for a more resilient and united team in the future.

7. How Can I Ensure Communication Remains Open and Effective Across Varying Team Dynamics?

Ensuring that communication remains open and effective across varying team dynamics is fundamentally crucial for the success of any organization. The first step in this process involves creating a culture of openness and inclusivity. Encouraging team members to freely share their ideas, concerns, and feedback can foster an environment where everyone feels valued and heard. This can be achieved through regular team meetings, where open discussions are promoted, and anonymous feedback channels are implemented to ensure that individuals feel safe when raising sensitive issues. Such practices help identify and address problems before they evolve into more significant challenges, thereby maintaining effective communication flow.

Another key step is using diversified communication tools that accommodate different communication preferences and styles. For example, some team members prefer face-to-face video calls for personal interaction, while others might find asynchronous communication like emails or collaborative platforms more effective. Various tools—from instant messaging apps like Slack to video conferencing software like Zoom and project management platforms like Trello—can help cater to different needs. This diversity supports various styles and ensures that communication remains consistent regardless of time zones or work schedules, which is particularly important in remote or hybrid work environments.

Training and development also play a significant role in ensuring communication effectiveness. Training sessions focusing on communication skills, such as active listening, clear and concise messaging, and non-verbal communication, can equip team members with the tools to communicate effectively. Additionally, leadership should model good communication practices, providing clear expectations and constructive feedback. Leaders can inspire their teams to prioritize open and effective communication by setting the standard.

Finally, regular check-ins and feedback loops are essential for maintaining open lines of communication across varying team dynamics. Scheduling routine one-on-one and group meetings provides ongoing opportunities for team members to share updates, voice concerns, and provide feedback. These regular touchpoints keep everyone informed and demonstrate a commitment to open communication from the leadership. Furthermore, implementing feedback mechanisms, such as after-action reviews or pulse surveys, allows for continuous monitoring and improvement of communication strategies, adapting them to better fit the team's evolving needs.

By fostering an inclusive culture, leveraging diversified communication tools, offering training, and maintaining regular feedback mechanisms, organizations can ensure that communication remains open and effective, promoting a collaborative and efficient team environment.

8. How Do I Balance Team Members' Differing Strengths and Weaknesses to Create a Cohesive Unit?

Balancing team members' differing strengths and weaknesses to create a cohesive unit requires an understanding of each individual's unique capabilities and how they can contribute to the team's overall objectives. This process begins with thoroughly assessing team members' skills, experiences, and personalities. Tools such as skills matrices, personality assessments like the Myers-Briggs Type Indicator (MBTI), and performance reviews can offer valuable insights into what each person brings. By identifying these strengths and weaknesses, leaders can strategically assign roles and responsibilities that play to each member's strengths while providing opportunities for them to grow in areas where they are less proficient.

Once the strengths and weaknesses are mapped out, fostering a culture of collaboration and mutual support is crucial. Encouraging team members to work together in complementary ways—where one's strength compensates for another's weakness—can lead to a more balanced and effective team dynamic. This can be achieved through team-building exercises, cross-training programs, and pair-work initiatives emphasizing collaboration's importance. Such activities help build trust, enhance mutual respect, and develop a sense of unity and shared purpose among team members, making the team stronger as a whole.

Effective communication is another vital component in balancing team strengths and weaknesses. Open communication channels encourage team members to share their challenges and seek help when needed, allowing for timely interventions and support. Regular team meetings and one-on-one check-ins provide opportunities for discussing progress, addressing concerns, and realigning roles as necessary. Leadership should model transparent communication and actively listen to team members' feedback, demonstrating their contributions and concerns are valued. This open dialogue fosters an environment where team members feel comfortable expressing their needs and leveraging their strengths.

Finally, investing in the continuous development of your team will ensure that the balance of strengths and weaknesses is maintained and enhanced over time. Providing access to professional development opportunities, such as workshops, training programs, and mentoring, allows team members to improve and acquire new skills. Encouraging a growth mindset within the team promotes the idea that everyone can develop their strengths and mitigate their weaknesses. This benefits individual team members and contributes to the team's overall competency and adaptability.

In summary, creating a cohesive unit from a group of individuals with varying strengths and weaknesses involves a strategic approach to role assignment, fostering a collaborative culture, maintaining open communication, and committing to continuous development. By implementing these strategies, leaders can harness the diverse talents of their team members, turning potential weaknesses into opportunities for growth and making the team stronger and more cohesive overall.

9. What Early Signs Indicate a Need for Reassessment and Refinement of Team-Building Strategies?

Identifying early signs that indicate a need for reassessment and refinement of team-building strategies is crucial for sustaining a high-performing and cohesive team. One of the first signs to look out for is a decline in team morale. When team members exhibit signs of disengagement, such as reduced enthusiasm, lack of initiative, or increased absenteeism, it may suggest that the existing team-building strategies are no longer effective. This decline in morale can stem from various factors, including unresolved conflicts or a lack of recognition, which must be addressed promptly to prevent further deterioration of the team dynamics.

Another early indicator is communication breakdowns. Effective team communication is essential for collaboration and efficiency. If you notice increased misunderstandings, missed deadlines, or unclear directives, it could signal that the team's communication channels or methods are not working as intended. These breakdowns can lead to frustration and decreased productivity, necessitating reviewing and adjusting the communication strategies to ensure that information flows seamlessly across the team.

A notable shift in team performance and productivity also warrants attention. When the team consistently fails to meet its goals or deliverables, it may indicate that the current team-building practices are insufficient to address the challenges. This could be due to ineffective role assignments, lack of necessary skills, or limited collaboration among team members. Evaluating the team's performance metrics and identifying any patterns of inefficiency can help pinpoint the areas that require immediate intervention and improvement in the team-building approach.

Additionally, increased conflict and tension among team members can be a warning sign. While some level of disagreement is natural in any team, persistent unresolved conflicts can hinder the team's ability to work together harmoniously. This may indicate underlying issues such as unmet expectations, perceived inequities, or personality clashes. Implementing conflict resolution strategies and fostering an inclusive environment where team members feel heard and valued can help alleviate these tensions and promote a healthier team dynamic.

Finally, a lack of innovation and creativity within the team may also suggest that team-building strategies need refinement. When team members are reluctant to share new ideas or take risks, it can stifle innovation and reduce the team's competitive edge. Encouraging a culture that celebrates creative thinking and providing opportunities for collaborative problem-solving can revitalize the team's innovative spirit. Regularly reassessing the team's needs and adapting team-building initiatives to support their evolving goals can keep the team dynamic, motivated, and effective in achieving their objectives.

10. How Can I Maintain Team Morale and Motivation During Significant Change or Uncertainty?

Maintaining team morale and motivation during significant change or uncertainty is fundamentally rooted in strong leadership and clear communication. Leaders must be transparent about the changes and their potential impact on the team. This involves providing regular updates, addressing concerns openly, and ensuring team members understand the reasons behind the changes. When leaders share information candidly, they build trust and reduce the anxiety that often accompanies uncertainty. Listening actively to team members' feedback and concerns is crucial, as well as demonstrating empathy and understanding. This two-way communication helps address apprehensions promptly and fosters a supportive environment.

In addition to effective communication, providing emotional and practical support is essential. Recognize that change can be stressful and offer resources to help team members cope. This could include access to counseling services, stress management workshops, or flexible working arrangements. Acknowledging the emotional impact of change and providing the necessary support convey that the well-being of team members is a priority. Moreover, practical support, such as additional training or resources to help them adapt to new processes or technologies, ensures that team members feel equipped to handle the changes confidently.

Another critical element is maintaining a sense of community and collaboration within the team. Encourage team-building activities that help members stay connected and support one another. This could be through virtual coffee breaks, collaborative projects, or social events. Building strong interpersonal relationships within the team can provide a buffer against the uncertainties of change, as team members can lean on each other for support. Promoting a culture of inclusivity and open dialogue where everyone feels valued and heard can further enhance team cohesion and morale.

Setting clear goals and providing direction can also help maintain motivation. During periods of change, uncertainty about the future can lead to confusion and a lack of direction. Leaders should articulate clear, achievable goals and outline the pathway to achieving them. This provides a sense of purpose and helps team members focus their efforts and energy on tangible objectives. Celebrating small wins along the way can boost morale and reinforce the progress being made despite the overarching uncertainty.

Finally, demonstrating resilience and a positive attitude as a leader can significantly impact team morale. Leaders who remain composed, optimistic, and solution-focused can inspire the same qualities in their team members. By modeling resilience, leaders can instill confidence in the team's ability to navigate the changes and emerge stronger. Encouraging a growth mindset and reframing challenges as opportunities for learning and growth can help maintain a positive outlook and motivate the team to push forward.

11. How Do I Effectively Manage Team Dynamics When Integrating New Members Into an Existing Team?

Effectively managing team dynamics when integrating new members into an existing team requires a strategic approach that fosters inclusivity, clear communication, and team cohesion.

Adding new individuals can alter the established group dynamics, challenging the existing balance and potentially causing friction. To mitigate these issues, leaders should prioritize inclusivity from the outset by ensuring that all team members, both new and existing, feel valued and included. This can be achieved by organizing introductory meetings where new members are formally welcomed and allowed to introduce themselves. Encouraging existing team members to share their experiences and insights can help bridge the gap between the old and the new, fostering a sense of unity and shared purpose.

Clear communication is paramount in this process. Leaders should clearly articulate new members' roles and expectations, ensuring that they understand their responsibilities and how their contributions fit into the broader team goals. Simultaneously, clarifying to the existing team how the new additions will add value and help achieve collective objectives is vital. This transparency helps to pre-empt any uncertainties or misconceptions and sets a positive tone for collaboration. Regular check-ins with new and existing team members can address any concerns promptly and facilitate smooth integration.

Building interpersonal relationships among team members is another critical element. Encouraging informal interactions, such as team lunches, social gatherings, or team-building activities, can help break the ice and allow relationships to form organically. Supporting mentorship or buddy systems where each new member is paired with an experienced team member can provide a structured way for new employees to acclimate. These experiences help foster trust and mutual respect, essential for a harmonious team dynamic.

Finally, maintaining a supportive environment that encourages feedback and continuous improvement is essential. Leaders should create channels for open communication where team members feel comfortable expressing their opinions and suggestions. This feedback loop helps to identify any integration challenges early and enables adjustments to be made proactively. Celebrating successes and recognizing contributions from new and existing members can further strengthen team unity and motivation. By continuously monitoring and nurturing the team dynamic, leaders can ensure a positive integration process that enhances overall team performance.

12. What Role Do Emotional Intelligence and Empathy Play in Successful Team-Building, and How Can They Be Developed?

Emotional intelligence and empathy are pivotal in successful team-building as they help create a cohesive and supportive environment where team members feel understood, valued, and motivated. Emotional intelligence, often abbreviated as EQ, refers to the ability to recognize, understand, and manage both one's own emotions and the emotions of others. It encompasses self-awareness, self-regulation, motivation, empathy, and social skills. In team-building, EQ enables leaders and team members to navigate interpersonal relationships judiciously and empathetically, fostering a culture emphasizing mutual respect and effective communication.

Empathy, a key component of emotional intelligence, plays a crucial role in understanding and sharing the feelings of others. It allows team members to relate to each other's experiences and perspectives, which can help mitigate conflicts and build stronger bonds. When leaders demonstrate empathy, they set a tone of compassion and understanding that permeates the entire team. This empathetic approach can lead to more collaborative problem-solving, as team members are more likely to support each other and work together towards common goals. Empathy also fosters trust, essential for open and honest communication within the team.

Developing emotional intelligence and empathy within a team requires intentional effort and practice. One effective approach is through training and workshops that focus on EQ skills. These sessions can provide team members with the tools and techniques to enhance their self-awareness, regulate their emotional responses, and improve their interpersonal skills. Role-playing exercises and scenario-based activities can help team members practice empathy by putting themselves in each other's shoes, thus gaining a deeper understanding of different perspectives and emotional responses.

In addition to formal training, fostering a culture of continuous feedback and reflection can also enhance emotional intelligence and empathy. Encouraging team members to share their thoughts and experiences regularly and providing constructive, supportive feedback can help individuals become more attuned to their own and others' emotions. Leaders can facilitate this process by modeling emotionally intelligent behavior, such as active listening, expressing appreciation, and addressing conflicts empathetically. Over time, these practices can become ingrained in the team's dynamics, leading to a more emotionally intelligent and empathetic culture.

Finally, creating opportunities for team bonding and relationship-building outside the usual work environment can strengthen emotional intelligence and empathy. Activities like team retreats, social events, and volunteer projects can help team members connect more personally and develop a deeper sense of camaraderie. These shared experiences build trust and understanding, which are the cornerstones of a successful and cohesive team. By prioritizing emotional intelligence and empathy in team-building efforts, leaders can cultivate an environment that enhances individual well-being and drives collective success.

13. How Can I Ensure Personal and Professional Growth Opportunities Are Available to All Team Members Equally?

Ensuring that personal and professional growth opportunities are accessible to all team members requires a multifaceted approach that addresses the diverse needs and aspirations of individuals. The first step is to create an inclusive environment where everyone feels valued and has an equal chance to succeed.

This means actively promoting diversity and inclusion within the team, recognizing and addressing biases, and providing support where needed. Leaders should intentionally try to understand each team member's unique backgrounds, strengths, and ambitions and tailor opportunities to align with those individual aspirations.

One practical way to promote equality in growth opportunities is by implementing structured development programs. These programs can include mentorship schemes, professional training, and continuous education initiatives accessible to all employees. Mentorship programs, for example, can pair less experienced team members with seasoned mentors who can provide guidance, share knowledge, and offer career advice. Regular training sessions and workshops can help team members acquire new skills and stay updated with industry trends. By making these programs available to everyone and encouraging participation, leaders can ensure that all team members have the resources they need for personal and professional development.

Transparency in career advancement processes ensures equal access to growth opportunities. Organizations should have clear, well-communicated criteria for promotions, raises, and advancement opportunities. This helps foster trust and ensures that all team members are aware of what is required to progress in their careers. Regular performance appraisals and feedback sessions can provide employees with a clear understanding of their strengths, areas for improvement, and actionable steps to achieve their career goals. Leaders should strive to provide constructive, unbiased feedback and support employees in setting and achieving their professional objectives.

Finally, fostering a continuous learning and development culture is essential for sustaining equal growth opportunities. This involves encouraging a growth mindset, motivating team members to seek out new challenges, learn from their experiences, and continually improve. Organizations can promote this culture by recognizing and rewarding learning achievements, providing access to learning resources such as e-learning platforms and professional development courses, and encouraging knowledge sharing within the team. Creating opportunities for cross-functional projects and job rotations can also help team members gain new experiences and perspectives, further contributing to their growth. By prioritizing continuous learning and providing equal access to development resources, leaders can help ensure that all team members have the opportunity to thrive and advance in their careers.

14. What Strategies Can Help Deal With Resistance to Change Within the Team?

Dealing with resistance to change requires a strategic, empathetic approach that acknowledges the concerns of team members while demonstrating the benefits and necessity of the change. One effective strategy is clearly communicating the reasons for the change and the expected outcomes. Transparency in communication helps to mitigate uncertainty and builds trust among team members. Leaders should articulate a compelling vision that explains why the change is necessary, how it aligns with the organization's goals, and the positive impact it will have on the team and the organization. Engaging in open dialogues, where team members can ask questions and express their concerns, further fosters an environment of trust and collaboration.

Another approach is to involve team members in the change process from the beginning. When employees are part of the decision-making process, they are likelier to feel a sense of ownership and commitment to the change. Soliciting feedback, considering input, and incorporating suggestions from team members improve the change initiative by leveraging diverse perspectives, increasing buy-in, and reducing resistance. Creating task forces or committees that include representatives from different levels and functions within the team can be an efficient way to ensure broad participation.

Providing adequate support and resources to help team members adapt to the change. This may include training sessions, workshops, and access to learning materials that equip employees with the skills and knowledge to successfully navigate the new landscape. Additionally, offering emotional support through coaching, mentoring, and regular check-ins can help alleviate anxiety and build confidence among team members. Acknowledging the challenges associated with change and providing encouragement and reassurance can significantly affect how team members perceive and respond to it.

Finally, recognizing and celebrating small wins throughout the change process can motivate and help maintain momentum. Highlighting successes and acknowledging the efforts and contributions of team members provides positive reinforcement and demonstrates that the change is yielding tangible benefits. This incremental approach helps to build confidence and reinforces the value of the change initiative. Leaders should consciously celebrate milestones and achievements, no matter how small, to keep the team motivated and engaged.

By implementing these strategies, leaders can effectively address resistance to change and facilitate a smoother transition. Building trust through transparent communication, involving team members in the process, providing the necessary support, and celebrating successes can help create an environment where change is embraced rather than resisted.

15. How Can I Leverage Emerging Technologies to Stay Ahead of the Curve in Team Development and Performance Enhancement?

Emerging technologies offer many tools and techniques that can be leveraged to enhance team development and performance. One significant way to stay ahead of the curve is by integrating advanced communication platforms and project management tools. These technologies facilitate seamless collaboration regardless of geographical location, allowing team members to work together more effectively. Platforms like Slack, Microsoft

Teams, and Trello provide real-time communication channels, file sharing, and task management features that help streamline workflows and improve productivity. Organizations can foster a more connected and collaborative work environment by adopting these tools.

Another key approach is implementing data analytics and artificial intelligence (AI) to inform decision-making processes. Data analytics tools can help track team performance metrics, identify trends, and highlight areas for improvement. AI-driven insights can predict potential challenges and recommend actionable strategies to overcome them. For example, AI-powered performance management systems can provide personalized feedback to team members, helping them understand their strengths and areas for development. Additionally, predictive analytics can forecast project outcomes and optimize resource allocation, ensuring teams operate at their highest potential.

Virtual and augmented reality (VR and AR) technologies also hold immense potential for team development. These immersive technologies can be used for training and development programs, providing team members with realistic simulations and hands-on experiences without needing physical presence. VR and AR can be particularly beneficial for complex skills training, offering a safe and controlled environment for team members to practice and refine their abilities. Furthermore, these technologies can facilitate remote collaboration, enabling team members to interact in virtual environments as if they were in the same room. This not only enhances learning but also strengthens team dynamics and cohesion.

Lastly, embracing continuous learning platforms powered by emerging technologies is crucial for sustained team development. E-learning platforms with AI and machine learning capabilities can offer personalized learning paths tailored to each team member's needs and preferences. These platforms can provide access to vast resources, including online courses, webinars, and interactive modules, making it easier for team members to upskill and stay current with industry trends. Encouraging a culture of continuous learning ensures that team members are always evolving, enhancing their performance, and contributing to the organization's growth. By leveraging these emerging technologies, leaders can create a dynamic and adaptive team environment capable of meeting the challenges of an ever-changing landscape.

Thank You

Thank you for taking the time to read this book. Your commitment to personal and professional growth is both commendable and inspiring. A

s you continue to apply the insights and strategies outlined here, we hope you find them valuable in fostering a more resilient, adaptable, and high-performing team. Remember, every step towards improvement, no matter how small, contributes to the larger journey of success.

We wish you all the best on your continuous development and excellence path.

www.ingramcontent.com/pod-product-compliance
Lightning Source LLC
Chambersburg PA
CBHW031622210526
45464CB00004B/1710